THE POCHAEV ICON
A Miracle in Our Times

With Akathist to the Most-Holy Theotokos
in honor of Her Wonderworking Icon of Pochaev

ARIANE TRIFUNOVIC MONTEMURO

Ideas into Books® WESTVIEW
Kingston Springs, Tennessee

***Ideas into Books*®**
WESTVIEW
P.O. Box 605
Kingston Springs, TN 37082
www.publishedbywestview.com

Copyright © 2023 Ariane Trifunovic Montemuro
All rights reserved, including the right to reproduction, storage,
transmittal, or retrieval, in whole or in part in any form.

ISBN 978-1-62880-306-8

First edition, October 2023

Please note that original spellings have been maintained
from all source materials.

Cover Design by
Ariane Trifunovic Montemuro.

Graphic Design by
Elaine P. Millen, TeknoLink Marketing Services, Charlotte, N.C.

The author thanks Holy Trinity Seminary, Jordanville, N.Y.,
for permission to use the Akathist to the Most-Holy Theotokos
in honor of Her Wonderworking Icon of Pochaev.

The Akathist is a translation based on the original Church Slavonic from
Saint Tikhon's Seminary Press, ©2002. Used by permission.

The author thanks Holy Trinity Store (https://www.holytrinitystore.com/)
for permission to use the image of the cross necklace
found on pages 11, 39, 69, 95, 125, 179 and 213.

(Psalm 135) Scripture taken from the St. Athanasius Academy Septuagint.
Copyright © 2008 by St. Athanasius Academy of Orthodox Theology.
Used by permission. All rights reserved

The author thanks her husband, Anthony Montemuro, M.D.,
for his editorial services.

Good faith efforts have been made to trace copyrights on materials
included in this publication. If any copyrighted material has been included
without permission and due acknowledgment, proper credit will be
inserted in future printings after notice has been received.

Printed in the United States of America on acid free paper.

Due to permissions and public domain issues,
the quotations in this book are from the King James Version
instead of from the Orthodox Study Bible except for Psalm 135.
See attribution above.

CONTENTS

Dedication v

Statement by Archpriest Serge Kotar 1

Introduction 5

Chapter One:
A Cross and a God-given Miracle 11

Chapter Two:
The Icon: A Holy and Transfigured Image 39

Chapter Three:
Tender, Loving, Ardent Intercessor:
The Mother of God 69

Chapter Four
Persistent Prayer and The Pochaev Icon Story 95

Chapter Five:
Holy History of Grace:
A Spiritual Hero and Battle 125

Chapter Six:
Our Cross and Our Miracle:
The Pochaev Icon of the Mother of God 179

Chapter Seven:
God's Miraculous Gifts:
Jordanville and its Pochaev Icon of the
Mother of God 213

Statement from His Grace Luke, Bishop
of Syracuse 229

Akathist to the Most-Holy Theotokos in honor
of Her Wonderworking Icon of Pochaev 235

From the Author 263

***This book is a fundraiser for Holy Trinity Seminary in
Jordanville, New York; it was completed in 2023,
the Seminary's 75th anniversary.***
*Please support the Russian Orthodox Church Outside of Russia
(ROCOR)'s Holy Trinity Orthodox Seminary by visiting,
praying for, or donating to:
Holy Trinity Seminary, P.O. Box 36,
1407 Robinson Road, Jordanville, New York 13361.*
***For more information and to preserve the future
of Orthodoxy, donate at www.hts.edu/support.***

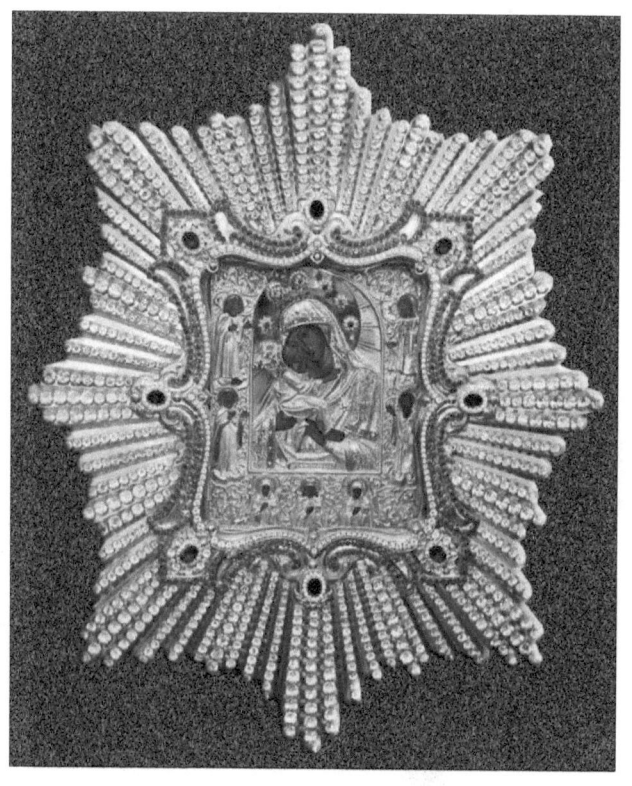

This book is dedicated to The Mother of God.
May She lead all of us directly into the arms of our Lord and Savior Jesus Christ.

The original Pochaev Icon of the Mother of God resides at the Holy Dormition Pochaev Lavra in Ukraine and is widely known for healing of the sick, helping in times of war, and many other documented miracles. The flow of miracles from this venerable icon continues to this day.

Troparion to the
Pochaev Icon of the Mother of God

(Tone 4)

We come as humble and sinful before the Theotokos

Falling down before Her Wondrous Image from the mount of Pochaev

With humility we gaze upon her and we fervently pray,

From the depths of our soul, we cry to our Lady and Queen:

O Most Wondrous Virgin, Mother of our Lord on High,

Who from ancient times hast taken the Monastery of Pochaev as Her habitation

Confirm this land in Orthodoxy and keep her in peace

And save us all who tearfully pray before this, thy Most-Pure Image,

Turn not away from us, thy servants, whose only hope is in thee. Glory…, now and ever…Amen.

THE POCHAEV ICON

Regarding the Pochaev Icon of the Mother of God

This book honoring the Pochaev Mother of God could not have been written at a better time. This sacred, miracle-working icon has its home at the Holy Dormition Pochaev Lavra in Ukraine. There are over five-hundred instances of miraculous intercessions done by this icon that have been recorded. How many more there must have been that have not been recorded!

At the time of this writing, a horrific bloody war is being waged between two brother nations, Russia and Ukraine, who descended from one root, Kievan Rus'. All human efforts on finding a peaceful solution which would end this bloodshed have proven to be fruitless. It appears that only divine intercession is able to bring this carnage to a stop.

All throughout Christian history, so many times it took the Mother of God to step in to stop war efforts. Wouldn't this be the correct time to seek intervention from the Mother of God to end this fratricide? This is especially true because the Pochaev Mother of God resides in the Pochaev Lavra, which is in Ukraine. This is especially true since in the past, prayers to this icon, along with prayers to the other divine intercessor for Pochaev, Saint Job, have already resulted in a tremendous miracle. In the seventeenth century an amazing miracle saved the Pochaev Lavra from destruction by Tartar invaders.

In July of 1675, hordes of Tartars under the command of Han Nurredin surrounded the Lavra from three sides and laid siege to it. There was no possible way to fend them off, as the walls of the Lavra were too weak to withstand an attack from such a powerful enemy. The abbot of the Lavra, Abbot Joseph, realizing that their only hope was in divine intercession, convinced the inhabitants, both monks and lay people, to plead to the Mother of God and Saint Job for protection. The people, on bent knees, pleaded before the Pochaev Icon and the relics of Saint Job of Pochaev. Their pleas were not in vain.

On the fifth of August, at sunrise, the Tartars planned their imminent attack and stormed the Lavra. The abbot with the people began praying, singing the Akathist to the Mother of God. Suddenly, at the sound of the first words of the Akathist, an image appeared above the church. It was the Mother of God spreading a white shining veil over the church. She was surrounded by a multitude of heavenly angelic warriors with swords drawn for battle. Standing next to the Mother of God and pleading for her to protect the Lavra was Saint Job.

The Tartars, in amazed confusion at this divine image, began to shoot arrows at the vision. Their arrows, in flight, turned back around at the same Tartars who were shooting them. Fleeing in panic they trampled everything in front of them, including their own warriors, trampling them to death. The defenders in the Lavra took off after them in pursuit and captured many prisoners of war. A number of the Tartars afterwards converted to Orthodoxy and remained permanently in the Lavra.

Having such tremendous defenders, it is inconceivable that the people in Ukraine have not already been pleading to their divine intercessors. But no help has been received to date. The reason for this may be that many other countries, with support from their citizens, are indirectly but powerfully participating in this evil war by supplying vast amounts of military aid to the war effort. This war has the potential to evolve into the third world war. All people in all nations involved in this conflict need to recognize how perilous the situation is and cry out for divine help.

This is why it is such a timely happening that this book is being produced now. As the late Archbishop Anthony (Medvedev) of San Francisco and Western America repeatedly stressed to me, there are no coincidences in God's world. The Pochaev Mother of God is a protector of Ukraine. I believe that as people read this book, they will find their hearts softened by the holiness of this icon. This could produce a groundswell of support by people to end the war. The icon has already profoundly touched the heart of the author of this book. May the Mother of God continue on reaching the hearts of all others.

— Archpriest Serge Kotar
Jordanville, New York, 2023

*The Magnificent Holy Trinity Cathedral.
A copy of Jordanville's Pochaev Icon of the Mother of God is
located above the royal doors.*

INTRODUCTION

The Pochaev Icon is one of many wonderworking icons in the Orthodox Church. A miracle-working copy is located in Jordanville, New York at Holy Trinity Monastery. It is wonderful to know that if you live in the United States, you do not have to travel abroad to see this icon in person. I wrote this book with the hope that each of my readers will profit spiritually by learning about and possibly even experiencing firsthand the God-given grace of the *Pochaev Icon of the Mother of God*.

I was also compelled to write a book about this miracle-working icon because the world is currently in a state of spiritual turmoil. This state touches each of us because the twenty-first century is filled with the spirit of the antichrist. We get daily doses of it. It drifts into our lives like a dense fog. We sense its darkness trying to eclipse our light. It infiltrates our homes. This vile spirit is the uninvited guest that pushes into our lives to shut our windows to Heaven. It wants us to forget God. The antichrist takes aim not only directly at us but also at our families. Our innocent and pure are its targets.

Because our peaceful lives are under attack, we are distressed by many things. It's easy to become confused or suddenly get despondent. In our ongoing struggle to keep our souls safe and secure in Christ, we pray that the peace of our Lord and Savior Jesus Christ returns to our troubled hearts. The bottom line is that we desperately need encouragement during today's spiritually trying times.

INTRODUCTION

Even one miraculous occurrence in our lives transcends the ordinary laws of nature and is transformative. A revelation of God's beauty and grace in life not only encourages but also deepens and renews our faith. Whenever I learn about someone else's miracle, or even encounter one firsthand, I realize one thing: these manifestations of God's grace must be shared to encourage and uplift those who love God.

Sometimes, these God-given miracles come to us in the form of icons. These holy pictures open our spiritual eyes so that we may be instructed and enlightened. Not long ago, while touring Holy Trinity Monastery with my family, Hieromonk Theodore (Stanway) mentioned something beautiful about miracle-working icons. He said an Orthodox icon is like an open window that helps us encounter the Heavenly Kingdom. Then Hieromonk Theodore pointed to the monastery's miracle-working copy of the Pochaev Icon of the Mother of God and continued, *sometimes God graciously allows a Heavenly breeze to come back to us through one of these icons.*

His comment struck me to the core. At the time of my encounter with the icon, I desperately needed to feel the grace of God. I was at the tail end of a cross I had been bearing for many years. I was caring for my bedridden mother in my home. Though no one else knew this, I did not believe I could do it anymore. I was beyond worn out. I needed spiritual encouragement and sustenance. My life was getting overcast and sometimes on cloudy days it is difficult to see and feel the Sun. However, in the presence of this bright and radiant holy image of the Pochaev

INTRODUCTION

The author with Hieromonk Theodore (Stanway).

INTRODUCTION

Icon of the Mother of God, I felt the refreshing grace-filled breeze the monk spoke of. I desperately needed this spiritual encouragement, and I will never forget this encounter with the icon.

The Heavenly breeze that touched my heart that day deeply strengthened my faith. I am only one of a multitude of pilgrims who has seen and been spiritually encouraged by this particular icon. This icon, a miraculous piece of material matter made of wood, paint, and a gilded covering (riza), is a portrayal of the transfigured invisible world of spiritual reality, of God and His Saints. It is a physical sign of God's grace. The holy image of the icon is a mysterious and miraculous bridge that comes to life through our prayers and longing for God. It connects the visible material to the invisible immaterial world. The theology *within* the holy icon is seen with our spiritual eyes. Simply said, the visible image of the icon leads the eyes of our heart to God.

All authentic Orthodox icons teach us something very important. They remind us that we too, can be transfigured. We can perceive a little foretaste of the divine glory and radiance of the Kingdom of Heaven, while still here on earth. These painted and/or carved gifts from God are not just for a few select people. *They are for every God-loving person.*

The icon which I am writing about here is one that you, too, can go and see in person, just like I did. God-willing, I will continue to visit this icon throughout my life. It is a miracle in our times… one of many that God, in His great mercy, provides for us. This beautiful icon is truly a bridge to the

INTRODUCTION

Heavenly Kingdom. It is for anyone looking to grow and deepen their faith. As an aid to achieving this spiritual aim, an Akathist to the Most-Holy Theotokos in honor of Her Wonderworking Icon of Pochaev can be found at the end of this book.

This icon is one of the most beloved images of the Mother of God. She is depicted tenderly holding Jesus Christ in Her arms. How Great our Lord and Savior is! He became small just for us. His Mother reaches out in her motherly compassion and intercessory prayers to keep all of us on the true path to salvation. She reminds us to remember Her Son, whom She served faithfully and spotlessly. Her life is the perfect example of how to be a servant of God. She teaches us to trust and dedicate our lives to the will of our Loving Creator. Her teaching is simple and clear: *Love Him, Obey Him, Follow Him.*

The loving, merciful, and tender intercessory prayers and supplications of the Mother of God to Her Son and our God on our behalf are an incomprehensible treasure for every human being. *She is the greatest of all the Saints* and therefore, *our greatest friend in Christ.* Her love for us is boundless. She understands our sorrows. She is our defender and helper. She is our compassionate Heavenly Mother. Best of all, She leads us step by step, rung by rung, up the ladder straight into the arms of Her Son.

I pray that the most wondrous and miraculous image of the Most Holy Mother of God from the Mount of Pochaev becomes a great and continuous blessing in your life! May the venerable and rich history of this icon touch your heart. May the bright and radiant Wonderworking Icon of Pochaev

INTRODUCTION

forever point you to a hope-filled life in Christ! After all, we can withstand all the assaults of the evil one if Christ is with us. The spiritual turmoil of this world cannot touch us. Joy and hope are ours; Christ is with us! *Indeed He is, and ever shall be*!

My hope is that some of you might even embark upon a pilgrimage to Jordanville to encounter the Pochaev Icon. Perhaps you will go as a result of reading this book. All I know is that because of it, my life has been changed for the better in every possible way.

"We magnify thee, O Most-Holy Virgin, and we honor thy precious Image which of old thou didst glorify at Pochaev."

— Ariane Trifunovic Montemuro
Nashville, Tennessee, January 2022

*The author with her husband and daughter,
touring Holy Trinity Cathedral with
Hieromonk Theodore (Stanway). The Pochaev Icon (without
riza) is located above the royal doors behind them.*

CHAPTER ONE

*REJOICE, O PRAISE OF POCHAEV,
THE HOPE AND CONSOLATION
OF THE WORLD.*

A CROSS AND A GOD-GIVEN MIRACLE

CHAPTER ONE

A CROSS AND A GOD-GIVEN MIRACLE

Suffering is part of a growing spiritual life. The path of life is full of pain, tears, and desperation. Difficult times can be the stepping stones to where God is calling us. It does us good to remember that our Lord and Savior Jesus Christ's triumph sprang forth from His painful Passion and Crucifixion. You may ask, why start our discussion with the difficult subject of sufferings or crosses we endure in life? The answer is simple. In our time of heartache and need, we yearn for signs that we are not alone. It only takes one miracle from God to bring us consolation. Our faith grows firm and the lanterns of our souls stay bright as we follow the narrow path to Christ.

This book which you are about to delve into is about the Miracle-Working Pochaev Icon of the Mother of God. The reason the book begins with the difficult topic of suffering is because the

CHAPTER ONE

spiritual beauty of the Pochaev Icon cannot be fully appreciated unless we realize one thing: Holy and beautiful things come to us by way of pain. Hearts washed by tears naturally draw near to God. Our dire straits can lead us into the eternal and immortal arms of God. In our suffering, we seek out the glory of His beauty. In our pain, we plead for His help because we are helpless without Him.

Our crosses rattle us enough to make us see we are not in control. We finally get it. Everything is in God's hands. God sees and directs everything in our life. After all, He is the Ruler and Creator of all. We should never despair. Even in the worst times in life, God is always at our side. We already know this, but it really sinks in when suffering is your constant companion.

The truth is God gives blissful rest, even in hardship. From generation to generation, the Lord helps believers who seek Him out. His divine providence manifests in various miraculous ways. One of these ways is through holy images or Orthodox icons. The icon is a holy object, the form being merely a receptable for the content; the content is determined by Holy Scriptures and the Traditions of the of the Church. That is why the work process is marked more by discipline than by inspiration.[1]

Since early Christian times, holy icons have marked the living path to Christ. The Holy

---

[1] The Mystical Language of Icons, page 12, Solrunn Nes, William B. Eerdmans Publishing Company, Grand Rapids Michigan/Cambridge, U.K.).

CHAPTER ONE

Orthodox Church has preserved its traditions regarding sacred phenomena since early Christian history. Miracle-working icons are part of this Holy Tradition. The holy image of the icon opens a Heavenly door. This in turn, allows for the manifestation of God's grace to work wonders. *Miracles happen when people pray in front of an icon.* The late Dr. Nicholas Zernov wrote that "icons are prayers enshrined in painted wood…" to "assist worshippers in their aspiration to Heavenly realm by actualizing the divine presence."[2] The Seventh Ecumenical Council in AD 787 defined the teaching on the icon. We have a dogmatic expression on Divine Incarnation and God's relationship to us and ours to God: "We confess and proclaim our salvation in word and images."[3]

Our faith is filled with spiritual treasures that help us endure the trials of life. It's easy to forget that help awaits us. God has graciously provided Saints for us to commune with. They are Heavenly friends that understand our tough times. Many Saints experienced unimaginable pain and suffering. They remind us how to pray and forgive. When things get really tough, we need friends like the Saints to show us the way. We need to possess the hope of His calling, and never forget that *God is here for us*. Therefore, we must remember the

---

[2] Wonderworking Icons of the Theotokos, 2nd Edition, pages 7 and 8, translated and compiled by Feodor S. Kovalchuk, publisher: Central States Deanery of the Patriarchal Parishes of the Moscow Patriarchate, Redford, Michigan).

[3] Ibid, page 8.

appeal of Saint Paul when he calls us to awaken from our forgetfulness:

"The eyes of your understanding being enlightened, that ye may know what is the hope of His calling and what are the riches of the glory of His inheritance in the saints." (Eph 1:18, KJV)

Even faithful believers yearn for a sign of His hope. Miraculous manifestations are sometimes needed in order for us to get up and face our crosses every day. Sometimes we become despondent and our spiritual eyes close. We are worn down and tired and we quickly forget the riches of His glory! When we fit into this category of forgetfulness, we are called to be grateful that God has not forgotten us. Time and again, He gives us the chance to wake up and remove the veil over our spiritual eyes. The manifestation of God's grace that takes place in prayer before an icon strengthens our faith and opens our spiritual eyes.

God enlightens those who have endured the fiery furnace of suffering and will give us understanding. Suddenly, we remember that our Creator loves us. He will help us. Why? Because in our pain, tears, and suffering we turn to God. Our hearts open. In our struggles, we inevitably start looking for *a sign from God*. The reason is simple. We desperately need Him. The pain we experience opens us to the mystery of holiness. In our fatigue, tears, and desperation, we come to know that God is always with us.

The subject of personal suffering is a mystery of great proportions. It is the enigma that is difficult

CHAPTER ONE

for any of us to understand. All we know is the journey to salvation is never an easy one. We need God every step of the way because these crosses we endure present us with so many unending challenges. Thankfully, our faith teaches us that our crosses bear spiritual fruit. They prepare us for eternity.

We try our level best to endure each challenge in our lives. However, to be honest, sometimes, we just cannot endure anymore. We are so tired. The last thing we need is to hear is someone telling us that the struggle we are enduring is for our eternal salvation. We already know that. We just want to make it through the day. We need to feel God's grace more than hear spiritual advice that has already been given.

Sometimes even prayer no longer comes easy. The words are not even there. It's all been said before—especially by those of us who are enduring a long-term struggle. Sometimes, all you can do is weep, sit in front of your icons, and say: help me Lord to make it through this, I cannot do it anymore. When you are in such a state, you really need a tangible sign from God.

You need to know you are not struggling alone. You want God to console your sorrowful heart. We need to feel encouraged by His love, peace, and presence in our life.

I often hope for such a sign of God's grace during my difficult times. One meant especially for me. More often than not, in despondency I whisper, where are you, God? Maybe some of you can relate. I strive to remember the continual presence of God

CHAPTER ONE

who is always there for me. I am inspired by David's words: **"I have set the LORD always before me; Because He is at my right hand I shall not be moved. (Psalm 16:8, KJV)**

I had a particular cross in life that directly led me to write this book. Without it, I am sure I would not have noticed the wellspring of holiness of the Pochaev Icon. Interestingly enough, the year the bearing of my cross began, God gave me a sign when I saw the words "The Pochaev Icon" in a dream. At that time, I had never heard of the word Pochaev, and had never visited Jordanville, New York. Quite frankly, I didn't have any idea what the word Pochaev even meant. I don't remember having ever seen it before. Thankfully, since my dream was so unusual, I decided to document it in my journal. Flash forward eleven years. When I stumbled across this written record of my dream, it became my miracle. But first, allow me to explain my ongoing struggle, so you can understand why I desperately needed a sign from God.

As a young woman, I always thought elderly lives were filled with a relaxing retirement, admirable wisdom, and the happiness of enjoying your grandchildren. However, I vividly remember my late father-in-law, Justice Frank J. Montemuro, often saying *"You'll rue the day when you are old and gray."* When I first heard this, I thought he said *"rule the day."* I must admit I was absolutely wrong about what he actually meant. The phrase he was saying was not *"rule;"* it was *"rue"* the day when you are old and gray. Shakespeare made this phrase famous. It means you bitterly regret the moment. One day

CHAPTER ONE

The author and her mother at the onset of her mother's illness.

CHAPTER ONE

I figured out — with the help of my husband — what my father-in-law was really saying. Now, I understand the difference between rule and rue. Not only am I entering those advanced years myself, but also, I began writing this book during a difficult time in my life.

At the time I began writing, I had been caring for my ninety-year-old mother Danica for eleven years, the last six of which she had been totally bedridden and unable to do anything. To say I was emotionally and physically exhausted is an understatement. I could barely muster up energy to care for her anymore. I had had countless difficult challenges caring for her. The journey had been a joyful sorrow. On the one hand, I had my mother; on the other, I did not.

I will say some positive things happened during this caregiving journey. It forced me to stay home with her, for instance, and as a result, I began writing this, my fourth book. However, like any cross in life, caring for my beloved mother took its toll. Especially during the years when she was entirely bedridden and needed 24/7 care, I struggled between managing her needs and my own family life. I am a wife and mother of two kids. My youngest child was only five and my oldest ten when my mother became ill. Back then I was forty-seven. Now I am fifty-nine. I had never gone to therapy for caregiver burn-out, but I knew I was at the end of my rope.

As I observed my mother over the decade of her health struggles, I was always in awe of her will to live, even when she became bedridden for the last six

CHAPTER ONE

years. I sensed her underlying spiritual strength. At one point, Serbian Bishop Longin came to visit her in my home and blessed her. After this, he pulled me aside and told me that my mother was enduring a *spiritual podvig*. This Russian term means *spiritual struggle*. The Bishop was basically telling me that my mother was drawing near to Christ. Mommy was traveling on the road to salvation. I was so happy to hear this. It was a miracle in and of itself that the Bishop from Chicago came to Nashville during that time, and while he was here, visited Mama.

His visit was a gift from God that encouraged both of us to endure. Neither one of us would have made it thus far without God and His Saints. I saw how Mama stared at her icon wall while in bed and looked at all the Saints depicted there as if they were living people. It was as if she was listening to them speak. And why not? They are real and are alive in Heaven! I believe my mother now knows the Saints far better than I do. God has a spiritually edifying plan for my mother that is still unfolding.

It is beyond my comprehension to imagine how anyone could lay in bed for six years. I could not last one week. However, if I reflect upon the deeper meaning of life, I can already see the spiritual fruits of this cross which I continue to bear. The buds are clearly there. Throughout all the difficult years, my longing and love for God has grown. It has become so great, I cannot fully express it in words. I finally understand everything begins and ends with God. My faith has strengthened tenfold. I know I am unable to do anything without Him. *I know I am nothing without God.*

CHAPTER ONE

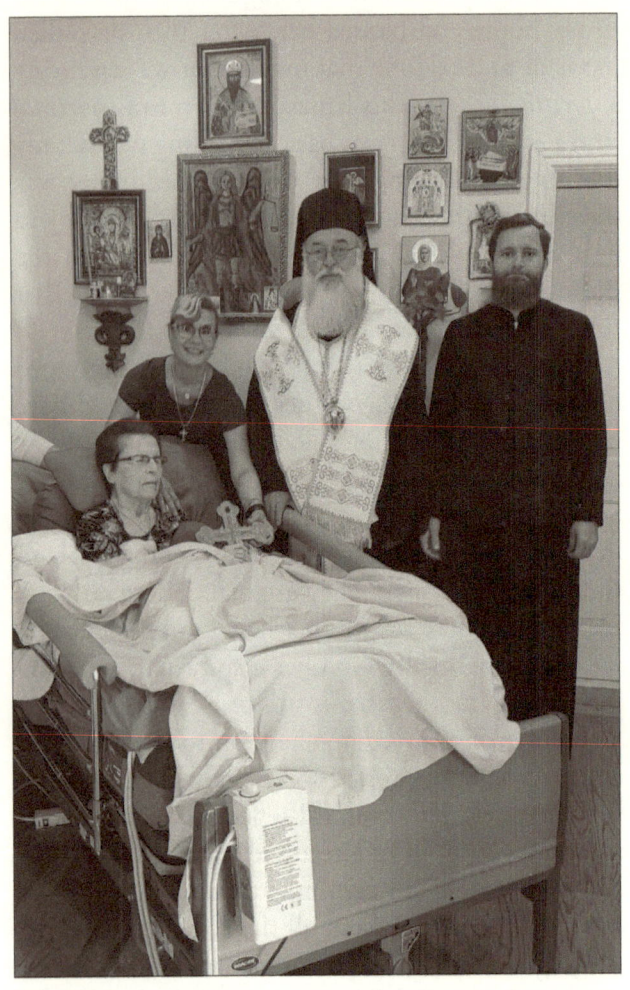

The author with her mother, Danica, His Grace, Serbian Bishop Longin, and Father Aleksandar Vujković.

CHAPTER ONE

Looking back, I can honestly say the only way I managed surviving that long caregiving journey was with the help of God. Thankfully, I had no idea, when it began, that it would be such a long and arduous journey. Along the way, Mama broke her hip and had to learn how to walk again. Imagine doing that with vascular dementia! She even survived a bout of COVID-19.

When this journey began my family was still young. All of a sudden, I was given another child, one who would be completely dependent on me for absolutely everything until the day she died. My mother had been a widow since she was fifty years old. I had no other family living nearby who could physically help me dismantle her life and care for her 24/7. *It was all on me* — at least that's what I used to think.

It took me years to figure out that what was really all on me was to completely *trust God to help me carry this cross* together with my mother. Each of us is a work in progress. I will always be working on the part about trusting God for every single thing in life.

I kept hoping somehow things would calm down during that caregiving journey, but that was not the case. A variety of dramas concerning her care always followed us; however, there were a few memorable days that really taught me to turn to God in anything and everything surrounding her care. After her initial downsizing move to assisted living, I was told within months to move her over to an even smaller memory care room. This required getting rid of another round of excess furniture.

CHAPTER ONE

Then one night after that particular move, someone from the nursing home called me around 2 AM. They said my mother was a code 342 or some such code. I had no idea what the code meant. The bottom line was that I had to come right away. I got up from my bed hoping not to wake my husband and kids. Then I dressed and got in my car. As I drove, I started to panic. *What would I do?* I am not a medical person. What could I do if she was dying? Thankfully even in my panic, my thoughts came back to God. God was with me. *What would God want me to do?* I wondered. He always teaches us to love, so I believed He would want me to go and love my Mama.

It was dark outside and in the facility. No one there would help me. No lights were on in the building. Only dead silence as I entered. A caregiver opened the doors quietly and stared at me. No greeting was spoken. I walked quickly in the direction of my mother's room. As soon as I got to her hallway, there she was halfway down the corridor. She was the only person in the endlessly long hallway. She was laying on a hallway bench. My beautiful Mama was completely naked with a tablecloth covering her. It was tied at the neck like a cape. I did not know if she was alive or not as I approached.

What happened next, I will never forget as long as I live. I ran up to her and exclaimed *"Mommy, it's Ariane. I am here!"* I knelt next to her, eye-to-eye level. Her chocolate-brown Serbian eyes opened and looked directly at mine. She said: *"Now I am nothing and nobody."* Knowing I am — *that all of us are* — nothing without God, without

CHAPTER ONE

hesitation the words just came, I took her hand and kissed her face and said: "No! God loves you, Mama! You are something and somebody in God's eyes, and He is with us right now! He made you special. You are a grandmother, a mother, a daughter, a granddaughter, an aunt, a niece, and most of all, Mommy, don't forget we love you! Now let's get up and go to your room and get dressed and I will stay with you until you fall asleep." So, she got up and squeezed my hand with love. We walked to her room. I dressed her and we talked, and she told me how proud my grandparents were of me and my brother. I kissed her and told her again how much I loved her, and she fell fast asleep. I have no idea how I knew what to say or how I calmly said what I said. But it's true. *We are all something and somebody with God!*

This holy exchange with my mother was a spiritual turning point for me. I will never forget how tangible God's grace was that night. It's been ten long years since that moment in time. I moved my mother three more times before she died. The last one of those moves was into my home, where I had designed and had an apartment added onto my garage for her to live in. When she had been there seven months, she fell and broke her hip. After surgery she was moved out of her brand-new room in my home to rehab, which is where she had to relearn how to walk. After coming home from rehab, six months later she suffered another stroke and became totally bedridden. It's hard to understand suffering, but God has a reason for everything.

CHAPTER ONE

Holy Trinity Monastery, Jordanville, New York

I marvel at God's will for Mama's life. Many people in the past approached me to tell me they were sorry to hear of her illness. They kindly asked if they could help me or pray for Mama. Now many of these people themselves have passed away. My cross constantly reminds me of who is in charge — and it's not me. Not only did God have a reason for Mama's long bedridden life, but only He knew in advance the exact day and time of Mama's last day. He created her. He had the final word.

I feel peace about where Mama is now. I believe God is with her. Now I want to do as God commands and honor her, even though with each passing year our cross was harder and harder to bear. I will be okay for a while, and then despondency slowly creeps into my life again. Deep down I know that when that feeling comes, hope fades and my eyes are closing to God. The good news is that throughout the years I have gotten better and better

CHAPTER ONE

Jordanville's copy of the Pochaev Icon of the Mother of God in a glass-enclosed cabinet (kiot) with jewelry displayed within its shadow box frame.

CHAPTER ONE

at recognizing when I need a spiritual respite. Not so long ago, I realized the time had come again to renew my faith.

Throughout the time of caring for Mama I discovered that visiting a holy place like Holy Trinity Monastery does wonders for my weary soul. Just hearing the bells ring at Jordanville gives me spiritual refreshment. I am smiling now even thinking about it. I literally feel God with me while I am there. Those of you who have been there or to other holy places can surely relate.

One recent visit, though, was a little different. I saw something I had never really noticed. One special icon pulled me in and prompted me to write this book. I remember the moment I first saw it and stood frozen in front of it. There was a sea of icons around me. The Pochaev Icon, however, was the only one that hit me like a hammer. It spoke right to my heart.

I immediately noticed there was something very special about that particular icon. As you gaze upon the shadow-box frame you see that many people have left a variety of jewelry behind at the base of the icon's frame. There was a predominance of rings, many of which look like engagement rings. Suddenly I felt such an outpouring of love and inexplicable empathy when I gazed upon each piece of gold or silver. My heart burst open. My curiosity was engaged.

I asked my friend Masha, who lives nearby, why there were so many rings and jewelry trinkets left in the shadow-box frame of this particular icon. She went on to tell me that in their desperation and

CHAPTER ONE

The author and her dear friend Masha Pavuk, standing in front of The Miracle-Working Copy of The Pochaev Icon of the Mother of God, Jordanville.

CHAPTER ONE

Close-ups of the variety of jewelry pilgrims have left behind.

CHAPTER ONE

searching for God's great mercy, love, and hope, people come from near and far to visit this particular renowned copy of *The Pochaev Icon of the Mother of God*. They come to offer their personal prayers or to ask clergy to pray before the icon, so the Theotokos can intercede and present each request to her Son. Masha went on to tell me about a woman who had tried over ten years to become pregnant to no avail. Then in her longing, hope, and desperation, she travelled to Jordanville to offer her petition in front of the Pochaev Icon. Not long after her visit her prayer was answered and nine months later she had a beautiful baby boy. She left her engagement ring in the icon's shadow-box frame in gratitude for her answered prayer. To this day, her ring resides at the foot of the Pochaev Icon at Jordanville.

As you gaze upon the beauty of these gifts, you can almost feel the suffering and tears people have endured in their lives. Each trinket left behind is a witness to God's grace. You cannot help but imagine the spiritual transformation that takes place in pilgrims' hearts while praying in front of this icon. I felt such love standing there that it was as if a door had opened to Heaven. In fact, I was so deeply touched, I could not stop thinking about this icon even long after I went home. Each piece of jewelry left behind honored our Lord. Each of them became a permanent testament to God's grace. Each is left behind for future pilgrims like me to see and become encouraged and uplifted by God's enduring love.

I pondered these trinkets and imagined each time I did how one person at a time turned to God

CHAPTER ONE

His Grace, The Most Reverend Bishop Luke (Murianka) of Syracuse, pictured here with the author at Jordanville.

CHAPTER ONE

with the crosses they bore. I, with my cross, was linked in a chain with their crosses asking for God's help, blessing, and mercy on each of our difficult situations. Our thorns were transformed into roses, so that now we each rest peacefully in the arms of God's limitless power.

My personal cross pulled me toward this icon, like a magnet. I was intrigued and felt befriended by every person who had left behind a piece of jewelry. In my heart it felt like I already knew these people. I felt their desperation. I felt their need for God. I knew that I was one of them because I, too, was struggling and knew their feeling — the need for God.

On the flight home, I couldn't stop thinking about this holy image of the Mother of God and the pilgrims who had left all their jewelry at the base of Her icon. My encounter had made such a profound impression on me that I immediately felt I had to write a book about it if I was granted permission to do so. Soon thereafter, His Grace, Bishop Luke, granted me the blessing to write this book. My heart filled with inspiration. I thought I would make the title short and simply call it: *The Pochaev Icon*.

Little did I know when I arrived home a surprise awaited me. One day I randomly decided to declutter some books in my bedroom bookshelf. I discovered an old journal from 2011 and amused myself by perusing through it before intending to throw it out. My eyes froze upon an interesting journal entry dated September 21, 2011 (September 21st is one of the feast days of the icon). I had written that I had dreamt of a three-

CHAPTER ONE

word name I had never heard of: *The Pochaev Icon*. Suddenly I remembered this simple dream. In it, I saw those three words clearly spelled out in front of me on a wall. And that was the end of it. I remember thinking what a unique word Pochaev was. I asked myself if there was actually an icon called Pochaev. I remember looking it up on my computer and then recording my curious dream. Little did I know that eleven years later I would fly to a Russian Monastery in New York and see this very icon in person. Nor did I know that my encounter with the icon would touch me so deeply I would eventually be inspired to write this book.

And now I am writing a book with the very same name as in my dream: *The Pochaev Icon*. How can one explain this? It is a mystery of God; only He knows the future. For me it is a sign that God is encouraging me, and He is with me. Sometimes when I doubt my ability to write this book, I remember my unusual dream. Remembering it gives me a boost of confidence. This is *my* miracle, a miracle God already had in the works just as my mother's illness began to take root, and before I had ever heard of, seen, or encountered the icon in person.

But God works that way. God works not only in particular moments, but these moments are linked. The Bible illustrates this. We see how the Old Testament links to the New and vice versa. To me, my difficult cross began with a gift from God in a dream: The Pochaev Icon. Back then, I had no idea what this three-word gift even meant. I remember I being befuddled by the spelling of the word Pochaev. At the time, I had never seen this word before, and

CHAPTER ONE

I certainly did not know this icon would encourage me during my difficult time of need. I remember being surprised there even was an icon with such a name. *Now I know all about it.*

Our yearning for God grants us the ability to sometimes experience great and holy beauty. My unique dream reminds us that when we are enlightened by our Christian faith, we possess the ability to discern and examine things much deeper than what is on the surface. This discernment sometimes takes time to fully understand. Isn't it wonderful how God gives us believers such beautiful spiritual consolation in our times of need.

Our Lord truly works in mysterious ways. How else could I have dreamed about an icon I would see in person and write a book about, eleven years later? On top of that I dreamt of it on one of its feast days! At the time of the dream, I had not written my first book; now I have finished three. Why I have not dreamt of the titles of my other books, only He knows. This is the eternal and immortal mystery of God. In His great mercy, He loves and encourages *all* struggling believers.

Remember how near the beginning of this chapter I said "Holy and beautiful things come to us by way of pain. Hearts washed by tears naturally draw near to God. Our dire straits can lead us into the eternal and immortal arms of God. In our suffering, we seek out the glory of His beauty. In our pain, we plead for His help because we are helpless without Him." The journey with my mother, the cross I bore, was the reason I was able to recognize God's miracle for me in The Pochaev Icon.

CHAPTER ONE

One thing I do know: God is always calling us and supporting us with His loving grace and timeless spiritual beauty. Soon it will be time to delve deep into the history and spiritual beauty of the subject of our book. But first, let's talk about what icons in general truly are, for each and every believer. Once we understand what an Orthodox icon really is, we will be equipped to fully appreciate the beauty of The Pochaev Icon in its entirety.

CHAPTER ONE

The author holding her beloved family icon of the Mother of God Pochaev in front of Jordanville's miracle-working one.

CHAPTER TWO

REJOICE, O PRAISE OF POCHAEV, THE HOPE AND CONSOLATION OF THE WORLD.

THE ICON: A HOLY AND TRANSFIGURED IMAGE

CHAPTER TWO

THE ICON: A HOLY AND TRANSFIGURED IMAGE

As we dive into a thorough understanding of the spiritual beauty of the Pochaev Icon, we start our discussion with a few basics regarding icons in general. Stepping into an Orthodox Church, we see icons or holy pictures everywhere. It is important to stop here and reflect upon the specific kind of image we are seeing in authentic Orthodox icons.

I grew up in a Serbian Orthodox household. As a result, icons are kind of second nature to me. To me, a house is not a home without icons. Years ago, I took several iconography classes with one of Russia's brightest lights, the Russian Master Iconographer Ksenia Pokrovsky (1942-2013).

Ksensia successfully imprinted upon all of us a deep love and respect for the great Russian Orthodox icon tradition. This was a priceless gift for all the students, even though an abundant majority of us never became iconographers — including me. Ksenia left us all completely in awe as we observed her teach and paint. I encourage each of you to learn more of this ancient tradition by reading the book *Hidden and Triumphant*, by Irina Yazykova. You will find Ksenia in this book. These classes with Ksenia taught me a tremendous amount about the history, materials, and techniques of iconography. I also became aware of how very little I knew about Orthodox icons before the classes began.

The author and her Russian Iconography teacher, Ksenia Pokrovsky. Ksenia courageously continued to paint icons even under the threat of Soviet persecution and arrest.

I will say though, what little I knew as a child still has value. As a kid and even now, these holy pictures continue to remind me that I am part of God's family. When I see icons of Christ and the Saints, I feel that I am not alone. I am reminded that help from holy people in the Heavenly Kingdom is

CHAPTER TWO

available for me. Even to this day, when I see an icon in my home it reminds me to pray. Our spiritual life and understanding of a specific icon prototype (such as The Pochaev Icon of the Mother of God) can benefit greatly the more we know about the Holy Tradition and meaning behind Orthodox icons.

First, let's start with a common misunderstanding regarding icons. We do not worship icons in the Orthodox Church. We worship God. We *venerate icons.* This means we show love and respect for the holy person we encounter in the icon. We kiss them in the same way we kiss relatives we love. We also light candles and vigil lamps and pray before them. When we look at an icon of our Lord, our prayers are directed to Christ, not to an icon. We do not, for instance, ask the icon of the Theotokos to pray for us; we ask the Theotokos Herself to pray for us with the help of the icon before us. Every icon exists to lead us directly to God. The truth of the matter is that an Orthodox icon is intended for the *act of worship of the one True God.*

Unlike a secular or worldly picture, the icon is a transfigured image of reality. In other words, icons portray the Kingdom of Heaven. The icon must also be a "true" depiction of the Holy Scriptures. Furthermore, everything portrayed within an icon must be derived from divine revelation and not from human imagination. An authentic Orthodox icon is always in concordance with the Gospel and Holy Tradition.

It is often said that icons do with color what Scripture does with words. Did you know that every single element in an icon has a spiritual significance and meaning? The icon exists to open the eyes of your heart for an encounter with the Heavenly Kingdom. There is a reason behind everything you see. Nothing is random. Everything you see in these holy images is depicted in a specific calligraphic and symbolic language. The brushwork, colors, composition, perspective, and so much more are used to describe this *transfigured reality*.

When you look at an icon you are looking into eternity. You will see a different perspective used in the icon tradition. It is called *inverse perspective*. We are normally used to seeing compositional lines converging on a point on the horizon. Instead, in the icon, we see that they converge on us, the viewer. The space becomes wide and unfolds in front of us. This allows us to step into the composition and be fully present with the subject. In this way, we feel included in the action depicted. We are literally drawn in.

The gold depicted in an icon is a symbol of divine light, truth, and glory. Iconographers use real gold leaf to convey this divine radiance because genuine gold does not tarnish with time. The icon shows us the magnificence of the Heavenly Kingdom where there is no darkness. Spiritual and divine nature is depicted in the icon instead of the human aspect of the flesh. For example, the transfigured person in an icon is saturated with the Uncreated Light of God. Therefore, they radiate light from within. An icon shows us a view of Heaven, so it is lighted by the Unchanging Light of God. Therefore, there are no shadows, or ways of showing day and night in these holy images.

CHAPTER TWO

Take one look and you can see that icons appear flat and not naturalistic. Again, there is a reason for this. When you are not following the positioning of three-dimensional space there is greater freedom to arrange things according to a symbolic and spiritual importance. Sometimes you even see a multi-view perspective in an icon. You can see the same person depicted more than once (at different chronological times) in the same image. Or you might notice that a person that is more important than another will be enlarged. All these techniques are done to make a spiritual point. Simply put, *icons are visual theology.*

The Orthodox Church has always fiercely fought to keep the purity of these sacred images. One of the rules of the authentic Orthodox icon is that it must be theologically correct. The battle was always about keeping spiritual decadence and secularization out of the holy images of the Church. These holy images are an integral part of the Orthodox Church. In an authentic icon, you receive the teaching of Orthodoxy. Instead of realistic beauty or artistic quality like secular art, the Orthodox icon gives you *Truth*.

An icon is not only an object of worship but a doorway to holiness and divine grace. However, its important to understand that prayer before any icon without faith in God, humility, or reverence, has absolutely no power. We must let go and allow God's will to take over. The Pochaev Icon of the Mother of God is often called a miracle-working icon. Throughout time, there have been many examples of these types of icons. Many still exist.

CHAPTER TWO

However, we need to remember that the icon itself is not miraculous.

Miracles are performed by God alone. He does use material things of this world (such as wood and paint) to help us share in the Heavenly Kingdom. We use water in Baptism or bread and wine in Holy Communion. We ask God to bless these ordinary things so that they can bring us to Him. That is why we also ask God to bless icons. This way the paint, wood, and the iconographer's skills can be used in His service. Icons are blessed with prayers to bring us to God. When we pray before these blessed icons, God always hears us if we approach Him in faith, repentance, and humility.

An Orthodox icon depicts Christ, The Theotokos (The Mother of our Lord), and His Saints as spiritually *transfigured* prototypes. The special word to make note of here is transfigured. Icons remind us that we too, can be transfigured. We can also experience a little foretaste of the radiance and Divine glory of the Kingdom of Heaven shining forth from icons. We can perceive this while still working on our salvation here on earth. The icon presents us with a holy invitation to open the door or window to the Heavenly Kingdom. Each of us can pass through this opening to encounter our Lord God.

This is where it gets personal. Do we feel prompted to open the door to God that the icon offers? Serbian Saint Nikolai Velimirović says, "Faith is nothing but a man opening the door of his soul and bidding God to enter." Our personal trials lead us to contact God. We desire to open the door. Our spiritual eyes

CHAPTER TWO

open and we see that icons are witnesses to Who it is, that is *"The Way, The Truth and The Life."* The Son of God became man. We can now depict Him. The icon, like the Word of God, is a way of knowing God. It is one of the means of contacting Him.

I know from personal experience that we begin to attach ourselves to God with greater fervor and frequency when personal hardships confront us. We learn that the spiritual fruit we receive from our difficulties prepares us for eternal life. Whatever we endure with hope and faith in Christ is priceless and can potentially save our souls. Ultimately, we try our best to remember that God allows us to experience all our challenges for the perfection of our souls. Perhaps our rational mind understands all of this. *However, enduring these crosses from day to day is a whole different story.*

Long-term care of my bedridden mother in my home has changed the way I look at life. Every day I encounter a sobering sight. Someone I love dearly laying helpless in bed. I see someone before me who can no longer do anything. My mother was once a vibrant and quite independent person. She now depends on me for all her physical and spiritual needs. My fear kicks in if I think about the future and Mama's care too much. I try to keep my faith strong and fight the urge to complain about this trial. I have no choice but to endure with faith and love in God's will.

When you are put in such circumstances, you ponder your own immortality. Fear becomes your companion. You wonder if you will be the next one down the line laying helplessly in bed. Outside

CHAPTER TWO

opinions stream in. I remember medical advice I received almost seven years ago. Prepare yourself, Ariane. Your mother is near the end. Funny thing is I heard this advice many times throughout the years. However, Mama is still here. Only God knows her time to go. Listening to the outside world and its opinions stresses me to no end. My mind often races with worry. I have never seen anyone die before.

The author's icon of Jesus Christ by the hand of iconographer Marek Czarnecki. Czarnecki trained under Ksenia Pokrovsky.

CHAPTER TWO

The more frazzled I became the more I did not know what to do. So, I began to call upon God for help. Every day I began to habitually light the flame in front of my icons. Rain or shine I began to pray more frequently. Doing this every single day always makes me feel better. Honestly, my worries still return. When they do, I try to fight them off with prayer. Not too long ago, I remember weeping endlessly in front of my icons. I kept saying God I cannot do it anymore. Help me, Lord. *All I have is you.*

During this time of desperation almost six years ago I discovered a beautiful prayer. After I pray these holy words, my worries stop dead in their tracks. I light my icon lamp, and I repeat the prayer directly in front of my icon of Christ. Before I begin, I face the icon and say, "I want to serve you, *Lord. Don't let my mother suffer. Please give me the strength to continue to care for her.*" I am so tired of taking care of my mother and trying to balance my family responsibilities. I often still silently wonder why He gave Mama her incapacitating stroke. But I leave my question behind as I stand before my icon and begin to pray. To this day, this special prayer comforts and strengthens me:

> O Thou who willingly dost give thy flesh to me as food,
> Thou who art a Fire, consuming the unworthy,
> Consume me not, O my Creator
> But rather pass through all my body parts,
> Into all my joints, my reins (the mind), my heart.

CHAPTER TWO

> Burn thou the thorns of all my transgressions,
> Cleanse my soul and hallow thou my thoughts.
> Make firm my knees, and my bones likewise;
> Enlighten me wholly in thy fear;
> Ever shelter me, and guard and keep me
> From every soul-corrupting deed and word,
> Chasten me, purify me, and control me;
> Adorn me, teach me, and enlighten me.
> Show me to be a Tabernacle of thy Spirit only,
> And in no wise the dwelling place of sin,
> That from me, thy habitation, through the
>   entrance of thy Communion,
> Every evil deed and every passion may flee as
>   from fire.
> As intercessors I bring to thee all the Saints,
> Both the Angelic Leaders of the Bodiless Powers,
> Thy Fore-runner, and thy wise Apostles;
> And besides these, thine immaculate and
>   chaste Mother;
> Do thou accept their prayers, my Christ, who
>   art Compassionate,
> And make thy servant to be a child of the light:
> For thou alone, Good Lord, are the sanctification
>   and splendor of our souls,
> And to thee as God and Master, day by day,
> Duly we all ascribe glory.
>   — by Saint Simeon Metaphrastes

The more I turned to God the more I was feeling the reality of our cross. Mama was not getting any better. God kept reminding me that I did not end up by chance in that position. He controls the circumstances of our lives. His will governs all. Mama and I were allowed our difficulties by God for the benefit of our souls. I began to pray more and talk to people less about Mama's issues and my fears. I began to accept my tribulations and to stop asking God: *Why*. Instead of giving in to fear, I told God my worries. Every morning I would get up and strive to trust Him. I still try to yield to Him and accept His will peacefully, even now. It's not easy, but I am getting better. Even to this day I continually remind myself, *God should always be your best friend*, Ariane.

My spiritual eyes open at certain moments, when I realize the only way I can survive is with God. A transformation takes place within my soul. My spiritual eyes open, and I begin to desire Him again. The light of the Heavenly Kingdom begins to pull me like a magnet. Without the cross my mother and I shared, I am convinced I would never have noticed The Pochaev Icon in the deeply personal way that I have. *My mother's and my holy journey together is why the holy image spoke to me.*

I distinctly remember the exact moment. It was near the end of my mother's last year. I was worn down and despondent, and was spiritually and emotionally and physically depleted. I was experiencing caregiver burnout. In need of a change of scenery, I needed to be reminded once again that God was with both my mother and me. Another pilgrim and I decided to go to Jordanville, where I hoped to find spiritual respite and refreshment. I was hoping for a sign of God's grace.

CHAPTER TWO

My family could see I was exhausted and encouraged me to go. Over the years my husband had often reminded me to strive to approach my caregiving journey with Mama like an endurance athlete, periodically repeating a helpful idea. He would say, "Remember, Ariane, this is a marathon, not a sprint." I reflected upon his idea often. It helped me pace myself. Even now, with more than ten years of caregiving under my belt, I still struggle with balance and self-care.

At the point that my friend and I decided to go to Jordanville, truth be told, I was beyond tired. I was desperately needing a sign from God. I needed encouragement from Him to continue. I was thirsting for refreshment from His Life-giving waters. After all, my caregiving journey with Mama truly was a spiritual marathon. I wanted to stay on track and make it to the finish line *with God* — not without Him.

I first saw The Pochaev Icon while touring the monastery, not long after I arrived. After the tour, I remember going back and standing alone before it. To my tired eyes, the Mother of God of Pochaev appeared absolutely beautiful and radiant. I felt glued to my spot in front of Her. I did not want to move. It was as if The Most Holy Mother of God was waiting for me. As if a personal invitation had been given. *Come, Ariane, take refuge in the living presence of the Heavenly Kingdom.*

I gazed at The Pochaev Icon in reverence and awe; then I looked down. At that point, I noticed something surrounding the icon itself. The base of the shadow-box frame was filled with a variety of rings,

CHAPTER TWO

crosses, and all sorts of precious jewelry. Suddenly I realized all these treasures were left behind by people *just like me* — people enduring their own crosses. I imagined them coming with tired hearts and heavy burdens just like mine. Maybe they were facing a health challenge. Or maybe they wanted children and could not conceive. Or perhaps they had lost their faith or will to live. As I looked over every single piece of jewelry one by one, I felt deeply connected to all those pilgrims and through them, to God's love.

Each and every one of those trinkets represents a person. Even though I never met any of them, I already knew them. I understood their need for help and consolation from God. I imagined them coming in desperation and praying before The Pochaev Icon and their prayers being answered. In time, I learned more about a few of these people and their miracles.

Once their prayers were answered, some of those pilgrims returned to Jordanville, where they gave thanks for their miraculous blessings. I was overwhelmed by the realization that many of them had brought their own precious jewelry to leave behind as a witness to their faith and their gratitude to God. Each piece of jewelry given by a grateful God-loving pilgrim now resides in the shadow-box frame which holds the wonder-working Pochaev Icon of the Mother of God. Every one of those pieces of jewelry represents hope, joy, and holiness. Each piece shines in the light of God's immeasurable grace, and because of them my heart smiles. You, too, can visit this icon and see these

CHAPTER TWO

precious testimonials from the people whose lives have been changed. No matter where you are in life, if you draw near with faith, hope, and love, the Heavenly Kingdom is within reach. *God hears you.*

This image of The Pochaev Icon of the Mother of God can be your holy gateway to know God. Even to this day, pilgrims like me come with their burdens. They come from near and far and pray before the icon. Their faith grows. Sometimes they even receive miraculous answers to their prayers. These testimonies are a great inspiration and spiritual gift for each of us. They show all of us how — even in hardship — we must continue to strive with love to unite with our living God.

Their miracles remind me that I am nothing without God. Even when I am desperate, I must fight to know Him better. Instead of asking *Why me?* I should thank God for any tribulation He sends my way. My struggle with Mama has brought me closer to Him. I must remember to trust Him. My sorrows have made me turn to Him. My Lord is my teacher and my guide. Most importantly, He is *my hope.* The miraculous Pochaev Icon manifestations also inspire me to fight against despondency. My faith in God weakens when I feel sorrowful and hopeless. This is when my spiritual eyes close.

My everyday caregiving burdens worried and sometimes frightened me. I tried to solve every problem in Mama's care myself. I forgot to ask God to show me the way. Thankfully, God repeatedly allows me the chance to return to Him and re-open my spiritual eyes. When they are open, peace returns. As a result, I remember to look to Him for

CHAPTER TWO

everything. My eyes become firmly fixed on the Heavenly Kingdom.

After all, the Heavenly Kingdom is our true home — *not the earthly*. This reminds us why the icon is a holy image. The Pochaev Icon is a meeting point. It is an intersection between Heaven and earth. Each of The Pochaev Icon pilgrims detached themselves from earthly cares, and sought to attach themselves to God. They brought their burdens to the Lord. While praying in front of the icon they stepped through the door into the Heavenly Kingdom. In their time of need, their hearts found this holy meeting point.

My mother's life perfectly illustrates how icons accompany the Orthodox Christian from birth to death. Icons followed Mama every step of the way. They went from her home, to hospital, to rehab, to nursing home, and eventually to her final room in our home. When Mama eventually died, I even placed The Orthodox Icon of the Resurrection (Pascha) in her hands for her journey to her final resting place.

I remember the sad day when she had her massive stroke. It incapacitated the left side of her body. It was devastating. The stroke rendered her completely bedridden from that time forward. A whole new way of physically caring for her began. Six years later, she was still in the very same bed right in my home.

After that happened, the thought came to me that I needed to help Mama pray. Like any of us, she also needed spiritual nourishment — not only physical care. After all, she was a living soul. I wondered how I could do this. The idea came to me to try to get

CHAPTER TWO

Mama to face each icon in her room. Then it hit me. Her hospital bed was on wheels, so I could easily move her. I began to roll her bed around, facing it in different directions. She had a large wall filled with many icons. I lined her bed up to face specific icons at different times. Then I began to talk to her about each one. I often reminded her that God and the Saints are alive, and she could talk to them in her thoughts because they could all hear her. I always ended our icon encounter with a short prayer.

This is how our little weekly prayer routine began. It continued until the day she died. I found great comfort in doing that with Mama. As her primary caregiver, I, too, needed a regular dose of spiritual strength to keep going. Our little icon prayer routine kept reminding me not to stress so much over her care. It also helped me remember that God is, and has always been, with me on this long and arduous journey. I always told Mama to trust God's will to endure her cross.

The irony is that sometimes I forget to genuinely trust God myself. I keep trying to control things. I could not change my mother's journey, or even mine for that matter. All I know is that it's a never-ending lesson for me to trust God, still, just as Mama had to on her own journey.

As Mama's body slowly faded away, one thing was crystal clear to me. The icons surrounding my mother were serving a holy purpose. They kept the Heavenly Kingdom in full view right before us, by ministering to our souls. Mama's icons reminded me to talk to her about God and keep Him at the center of our lives. I am thankful that a Serbian priest came to give Mama communion once a month. I am also grateful for my mother's icons, because they were a source of spiritual strength for both of us. They reminded me to pray with her as we endured our cross together.

The problem I still face, after all these years, are my frazzled nerves. All the daily responsibilities

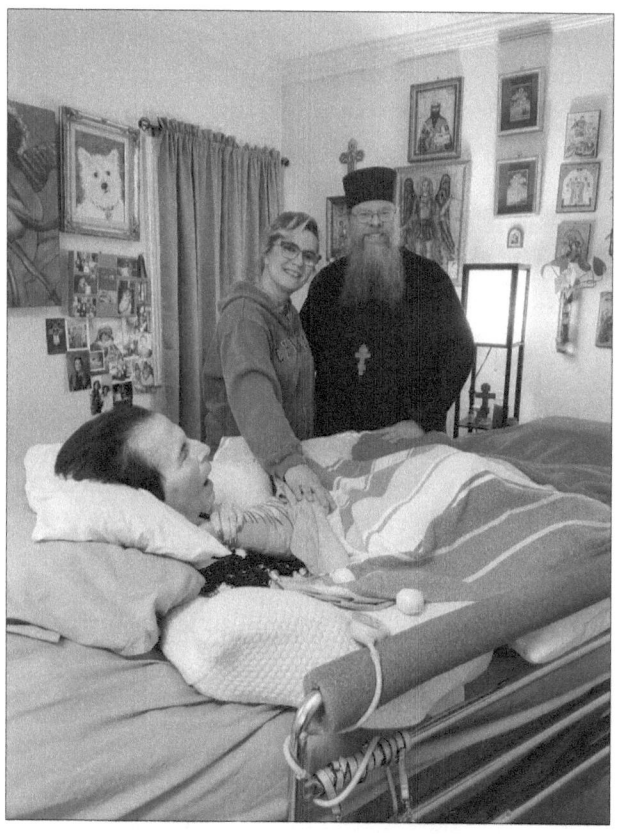

The author with her mother and ROCOR (Russian Orthodox Church Outside of Russia) Priest, Very Reverend Father Christopher Stanton.

CHAPTER TWO

surrounding my mother sometimes piled up and threw me off balance. The details of caring for her seemed unending. All the supplies (diapers, bedding, medications, etc.), her ever-changing meals, overall hygiene (including dental), exercising of mind and body. I always wondered what I forgot to get or do for her. Plus, I could not ignore life with my kids and husband. Many times, I caught myself pondering how much longer we had to endure that cross together. What's even worse is that when frustration sets in, I still ask God sometimes, why. At least now when this happens, I know to go light my icon lamps, cross myself and pray before the icons in my home. Peace returns to my troubled heart.

Time and time again, these holy images come to my spiritual and emotional rescue. God's grace illuminates each one. Every time I entered Mama's room, I made sure the flame was on before her Icon of Christ. I often bought battery-operated tea lights, so the flame was never out. This was not only for her, but also for me. Seeing the glowing flame before the icons helped me let go of all my earthly cares. I kept telling myself, *God has this, Ariane. It is in His Almighty hands.* The icon flame flickered. Then, once again, I remembered to attach myself to God. I relaxed into knowing God is with me and my worries began to leave the room. Icons radiate the strength, hope, and peace of God. They reminded me then and now that I am never alone.

I understand that hearing is the last physical sense to go before one passes. At that point in our journey, some days Mama was with us — other days not so

CHAPTER TWO

much. Even on the days when her eyes were closed, I talked directly to her soul. I strategically placed my mouth near her ears and talked to her about the Heavenly Kingdom. I asked her to imagine the beauty that awaits those who love God. I told her to follow God by letting go of grudges. I asked her to think of anyone she might have wronged and forgive them. We had nice little soul-to-soul conversations and sometimes, at the end, her eyes opened. Then I told her that the Saints are with us and that they were praying for her. I mentioned their names and occasionally Mama lifted her eyebrows in acknowledgment. Since she could no longer speak clearly, this little gesture made me so happy. I knew she could hear me.

Many times, I elaborated a bit more and described the Saints' life stories — especially those Saints on the icon wall near her bed. On her good days, Mama had some quite deliberate responses to my words. More than once I saw my mother smile and wave directly at the Saint on the wall that I mentioned. I even videotaped her doing this once. It was incredible. During the conversation she even mouthed unintelligible words to them. She talked to God and His Saints as real people. I am not the only one who witnessed her do this. Emotion poured from her face. I often looked twice because it felt as if there really was an extra person in the room with us.

One encounter particularly touched me deeply. As usual, I had turned her bed to face the large icon of the Mother of God and Christ. I told Mama *let's say Oče Naš* (The Lord's Prayer in Serbian) *together.*

CHAPTER TWO

She moved her right hand (the stroke impaired her left side) up to her chest. Then she grabbed the cross hanging on her neck chain. She proceeded to move it up then down and side to side, touching her chest in each direction. Clearly, she was crossing herself in prayer before the icon. I could not help but weep. Seeing this touched me in a happy way.

As you can see, I have seen firsthand the transfigurative power of the icon. An encounter with such an image is transformative. It literally draws one *into* the Heavenly realm. Day to day worldly cares slip away. From generation to generation, God continues to work miracles through material objects, including holy images. They must be perceived of and set aside from any other random worldly image. Icons must be approached with great respect. The *honor* given to an icon is referred to as *veneration*. When you venerate an icon, you open a door to holiness. An encounter has begun. You desire to know the Heavenly Kingdom. You are honoring and respecting God and His *friends* (Saints). These Saints eventually become *your friends* and lead you straight to God. The Church Fathers explain this perspective simply. They teach us that icons make present that which is represented. Therefore, the veneration of an icon is *an actual encounter with a person*.

This is when we must draw a line in the sand. We have to stop and understand what we are really seeing. It is clear that icons are *not just any image*. They are *holy*. However, this is where things might get confusing for the viewer. The very existence

CHAPTER TWO

of holy images in today's Godless world sounds unbelievable and almost impossible. After all, we are literally bombarded with worldly visual imagery every way we turn. In the span of each day, we absorb more visual imagery than words. This is because our brains consume and process pictures more quickly than text.

There are so many unremarkable worldly images that we see throughout our day, week, and year. To me, they all seem to blur together. They are mundane and forgettable. In our technological age, we do so many things at once. Always on the go, we are driven by a desire to process information quickly. For the most part, we no longer have the time to sit down and thoughtfully read through a book or newspaper. Instead, we would rather get our information by consuming video images at lightning speed. Our eyes encounter image after image non-stop. Our eyes, minds, and hearts perceive these as commonplace pictures. Because we are immersed in this overabundance of ordinary images, it becomes almost impossible to believe that holy images exist — even today. *The good news is the holy image exists in the form of the authentic Orthodox icon.*

At first glance, when you look at an icon, you see paintings, frescoes, mosaics, or carvings. However, you are not just seeing a decorative piece of earthly matter. An icon is so much more than its material form. Its inherent holiness distinguishes it from any other art form. A person can enter the mystery of God while praying before an icon. So, an icon is not just any image. It is a *holy* image. A holy image in a Christian mind is one set apart from

CHAPTER TWO

the realities of everyday life or more specifically our worldly life.

The word icon comes from the Greek term, eikona. Eikona means image, likeness, or portrait. Icons not only beautify churches, but these holy images are an integral part of the liturgical life of the Orthodox Church. Additionally, their presence sanctifies and brings holiness and prayer into *all* places — even homes, cars, and businesses. Once I even saw a photo of icons inside a space shuttle! You can be sure that when my son recently went off to college, I made sure he had a couple of icons in his dorm room.

The radiance and divine glory of the Kingdom of Heaven has been preserved throughout the centuries in the image of an authentic Orthodox icon. Throughout its ancient history, the Church has battled to keep spiritual decadence and secularization out of its holy images. In the early Church, this tradition of holy images was also shared with the Christendom of Western Europe. Around the fourteenth century, naturalism began to seep into Western religious art. The aesthetically-pleasing depiction of holy men and women began to emerge. In other words, the portrayal of realistic, emotional, and worldly beauty took over. Artists began to insert their ideas and opinions into compositions. The truth and the purity of the Christian sacred image was lost.

Thankfully, the Orthodox Church fought for and retained the holy image. We already know the holy purpose or goal of the icon is to give the believer the feeling that whatever is depicted in the icon is

CHAPTER TWO

present. However, we must pause and absorb what this really means. The subject portrayed in each icon is *alive*, like the Church, *which is the living body of Christ*. So, too, the icon must be *alive*. It must be a living presence in the Church. Over time a system of rhythmic and calligraphic visual language of painting principles was developed to achieve this goal. Color, light, perspective, and brushwork are all vehicles used to achieve this aim for the Church.

I love how every stylized brush stroke of an icon is painted (or carved) in prayer. While working, the iconographer prays: *Lord Jesus Christ, Son of God, have mercy on me, a sinner*. The icon opens our eyes to God and our true nature. The holy image in the Orthodox icon is an image set apart from our everyday realities (worldly life). How wonderful it is that God gives us free will to choose to have these types of holy images in our lives.

The Pochaev Icon — or any authentic Orthodox icon — exists for us to choose to encounter, participate, and commune with Him. With faith and love, each of us can open this door and enter in. We must keep in mind that the way one approaches an icon is distinctly different than any other image. I recall reading that a Saint once said that prayer before an icon brings an icon to life. Icons are therefore living parts of the Church. I also remember hearing stories of confiscated icons that had been stolen out of churches and placed in random museums. Even when non-believing visitors encountered these icons something unusual happened. They would feel the need to bow their heads and pray. Even people who have never seen an icon feel something uniquely

CHAPTER TWO

meaningful and deep. They feel a mysterious pull within their hearts. That is because these precious images are created and sanctified to serve a *holy purpose*. In this crazy world, icons give us hope of His Resurrection.

Sometimes it is difficult to let go of earthly cares. We might find it hard to recognize and choose the spiritual encounter an icon gives us. We need to quiet our thoughts with prayer and remember this temporary world is just an illusion and temporary refuge. At the end of time, when Christ comes again, we will rise from the dead. We will not look like we do now. God-willing we will be transfigured just like the images of the holy icon. I pray that one day my mother, too, will be transfigured and shine with the glory of God.

The icon's holy purpose is now clear. The time has come to delve in and explore the miracle-working icon and the subject of this book: *The Pochaev Icon of the Mother of God*. As we begin to study this icon, we see the Most Holy Mother of God directly facing us. She is tenderly inclining her head toward her Son. She holds Him in Her right hand. In Her left hand, She holds a napkin, with which She covers His feet. Christ is depicted imparting a blessing to those for whom He is *"the Way, the Truth, and the Life."* On the sides and bottom half of the icon you see miniature images of seven saints. These Saints were most likely chosen by the family that commissioned the icon. On the right, the Prophet Elias and, below him, the Martyr Menas, are depicted, while the Protomartyr Stephen and the Venerable Avraamius are featured on the left. Across the bottom the images of the

CHAPTER TWO

Great Martyr Catherine and Martyrs Parasceve and Irene. The Pochaev Icon is also covered by a golden ornamental *riza* (robe in Russian). This is a decorative covering that is used for both venerating an icon as well as protecting the painted surface of the icon from blackening caused by soot and smoke from the vigil lamps and incense used during church services.

The golden riza or robe covering the Pochaev Icon is a work of art in and of itself. Not only do we see bright gilt metal and precious gemstones, but

The Jordanville Pochaev Icon of the Mother of God with riza.

CHAPTER TWO

also this riza is magnificent in its workmanship and detail. When you study it in full color (see front cover of book) you cannot help but think this must be a very special icon to have such an exquisite covering. The riza covers almost the entire icon except for the Saints on the sides, the feet of Christ, and the hands and faces of the Mother of God and Son. It could be said that the riza made for The Pochaev Icon of Mother of God not only protects the holy image behind it but also honors what the icon represents: the Ardent Intercessor, Mother of the Lord on high and Her Son, Christ our God.

We will uncover more of The Pochaev Icon in the next chapter, where we discuss the spiritual significance of its main subject, the Most Holy Mother of God. The Theotokos is our bridge between Heaven and earth and the greatest of all the Saints.

CHAPTER TWO

A copy of the Pochaev Icon of the Mother of God (without riza) is located above the royal doors of the main altar at Holy Trinity Cathedral, Jordanville.

CHAPTER THREE

*REJOICE, O PRAISE OF POCHAEV,
THE HOPE AND CONSOLATION
OF THE WORLD.*

TENDER, LOVING, ARDENT INTERCESSOR: THE MOTHER OF GOD

CHAPTER THREE

TENDER, LOVING, ARDENT INTERCESSOR: THE MOTHER OF GOD

The beautiful *Pochaev Icon of the Mother of God* invites us to pause and reflect upon the great spiritual magnificence of the Theotokos. In this icon, we are not simply gazing upon a lovely and pious woman, for *The Most-Holy Theotokos is no ordinary woman*. She is a central part of the Incarnation. We are seeing the woman through whom Christ came into our world. Her pure life and immeasurable obedience to God offers us a shining example of Christian perfection. The Mother of God is the bridge between Heaven and earth. She did the unimaginable and gave birth to our Creator. From this mortal woman, infinity and immortality was born. An ancient Orthodox Church hymn expresses this beautiful truth: Her womb *"became more spacious than the Heavens"* by bearing the incarnate

CHAPTER THREE

Son of God. "He made thy body into a throne, and thy womb more spacious than the Heavens." Megalynarion (Greek), Velichaniye (Slavonic)

The All-Holy and Most-Pure Theotokos brought salvation into the world by bearing, nurturing, and following Our Lord Jesus Christ, who became man through His mother. The Church honors the Theotokos and calls for Her intercessory prayers and supplications to Her Son, our God. Her prayers for us are unlike any other prayers. They are extremely powerful prayers because of who She is. We must always remember that the Theotokos is *our Chief and Ardent Intercessor before the Throne of God.*

Orthodox faithful have been seeking refuge in Her intercessory prayers from the beginning of the Ancient Church up until this very day. Devotion to the Theotokos has always been an essential part of the Church's inner life. Early Christians recognized the Mother of God as a powerful intercessor for those suffering or in need of protection. One of the

THE PAPYRUS READS:	ENGLISH TRANSLATION
1 ΥΠΟ ΤΗΝ CHN	1 BENEATH YOUR
2 ΕΥCΠΛΑΓΧΝΙΑΝ	2 COMPASSION
3 ΚΑΤΑΦΕΥΓΟΜΕΝ	3 WE TAKE REFUGE
4 ΘΕΟΤΟΚΕ ΤΑC ΗΜΩΝ	4 THEOTOKOS OUR
5 ΙΚΕCΙΑC ΜΗ ΠΑ	5 PETITIONS DO NOT DE-
6 ΡΙΔΗC ΕΜ ΠΕΡΙΤCΤΑCΕΙ	6 SPISE IN TIME OF TROUBLE
7 ΑΛΛ' ΕΚ ΚΙΝΔΥΝΟΥ	7 BUT FROM DANGER
8 ΡΥCΑΙ ΗΜΑC	8 RESCUE US
9 ΜΟΝΗ ΑΓΝΗ, ΜΟΝ	9 ONLY HOLY ON-
10 Η ΕΥΛΟΓΗΜΕΝΗ	10 LY BLESSED

The translation of the earliest known prayer written to the Theotokos, written on papyrus in Koine (ancient) Greek, in 250 AD.

CHAPTER THREE

oldest known prayers to the Mother of God was found on a papyrus fragment dating all the way back to 250 AD.

As described in the Gospels, Jesus Christ was born of a woman — the Virgin Mary — and was a real human child who grew into a full-grown man. He is both fully God and fully human. Orthodox Christians worship the Father, Son, and Holy Spirit — *the Holy Trinity, the one God*. Jesus Christ is the second person of the Holy Trinity. He is the Savior of the world.

Saint John Maximovitch has said that correct Orthodox understanding of Mary the Birthgiver of God is essential for a right understanding of Jesus Christ, the Son of God. Orthodox Christians do not consider Christ's mother (the Theotokos) as a co-Redemptress along with Jesus Christ. Orthodox Christians do not honor a woman named Mary. Rather, we venerate Mary as the Theotokos — the Mother of God. She is an integral part of our faith and understanding the Incarnation of the God-Man. She can never be forgotten or ignored. Throughout our lives, it benefits us to often stop and contemplate Her greatness and profess exactly who She is. In fact, this is what the early Church did for us when they convened in the city of Ephesus for the Third Ecumenical Council. At this Council it was indeed affirmed that She is *"the Theotokos"* because She gave birth to Christ, a person who is both fully human and fully divine.

Our understanding of Christ and our Christian faith is an incomplete truth without the Theotokos. Think of it as a family portrait. How can you leave

CHAPTER THREE

your mother out of the picture? I find it comforting to remember that we all have a Heavenly Mother.

Most of us already know the basics about the Theotokos. However, even if we do, it's a good habit to frequently reflect upon Her spiritual magnificence. When we do this, our spiritual lives benefit. The fact is we get busy. We often forget about the Mother of God outside Church services. Little by little, the world takes over. Sometimes we remember to pause and thank God for our blessings. It is important to remember the Theotokos in our personal prayer lives. Many of us do ask for Her help, but do we ever stop to *thank* Her for all She does for us?

The Theotokos is our compassionate Mother and our greatest Intercessor. She ceaselessly pleads to God for each of us. When we are in need of quick and sure help, She is there for us. She hears those who honor Her. The truth is Her requests have boldness before our Lord. The perfect example of this gift of Her intercession can be found in the Gospel of John (2:1-11). This is the story of Christ's first miracle at the wedding of Cana in Galilee. When the wine ran out, She asked her Son for more wine. She asked for a public miracle. By doing so, She openly revealed to all that *He is the Messiah*.

We know what happens next: *He grants Her request*. Her intercessions for us have great effect. Her Son listens. Even to this day, the Mother of God continues to speak to Her Son on our behalf and is our Chief Intercessor before His Throne. Our souls benefit when we ask for Her tender maternal intercessions. She is Christ's first and best disciple. She leads us to Christ.

CHAPTER THREE

My favorite description of the person of the Mother of God is the one given by Saint John Maximovitch in his book, *The Orthodox Veneration of Mary the Birthgiver of God*. Saint John says there is no intellect or words to express Her greatness. Wow. That pretty much sums it up.

It's incredible to think how God the Father chose *Her*, God the Holy Spirit descended upon *Her*, and God the Son dwelt in *Her*. Think about that for a moment! God chose *Her* over everyone else on earth. I marvel at how Archangel Gabriel told Her She was about to be with child, *without seed*. On top of that, She *yielded to God's will* without questioning. I cannot imagine myself doing this without an emotional outburst. In the house of Elizabeth, She sang: "My soul doth magnify the Lord, and my Spirit hath rejoiced in God my Saviour." (Luke 1:46-47) The Mother of Christ teaches us how to be a true Christian. At the wedding of Cana, She advised the servants that "whatever He, my Son and my God, says to you, do it." The Theotokos points us to the Source of all life and reminds us to obey Him.

All her earthly life She proved worthy of the Heavenly Kingdom. As our Heavenly helper, She lovingly fulfilled the role given to her as Mother of Our Lord. She gave birth to Him, raised Him, and protected Him in the days of His youth. Christ also loved, respected, and was concerned for His mother. Even from the Cross, He instructed Saint John the Evangelist to care for Her. He simply said, *"Behold thy mother."* These three words are also said for *you and me*.

CHAPTER THREE

According to Holy Tradition, the first image of the Mother of God with Her Son was created by Saint Luke the Apostle. After Her death, the Apostles began to venerate Her not only as the Mother of their beloved Teacher and Lord, but also as their Heavenly Helper, Protector of Christians, and Intercessor for the whole human race before the Righteous Judge.

Everywhere the Gospel of Christ was preached, His Most Pure Mother also began to be glorified. Her earthly life was just the beginning of Her greatness. The Mother of God sees our every tear and hears our every plea. Because Her earthly life was filled with suffering, She understands our worldly cares and prays for us as our loving Heavenly Mother.

In the Orthodox Church, The Mother of God is considered the greatest of all the Saints. I like to think of Her as my Irreplaceable Helper. In Church we hear so many beautiful references that continually help remind us as to who She truly is. Here are just a few: ***"Life-Giving Spring and Joy of All Who Sorrow, Intercessor For the Offended, Feeder of the Hungry, Consolation of Travelers, Harbor of the Storm-Tossed, Visitation of the Sick, Protection and Intercessor for the Infirm, Staff of Old Age."*** My favorites are "The Mother of God Unceasing In Prayers" (*Kontakion of Dormition*), and "Saving the World By Thine Unceasing Prayer" (*Theotokion of the Third Tone*). Knowing all that She is, what a huge loss it is if we forget to ask for Her intercessory prayers.

CHAPTER THREE

Before her illness, my mother used to always pray for me. She would light a candle for each of her children and grandchildren upon entering Church. I miss having a mother who prays for me and my salvation. Saint John Chrysostom of the fourth century instructed mothers to consecrate their children through prayer. He also saw motherhood as a vocation that can lead to a Heavenly reward. His spiritual instructions inspire me to not only pray for my children, but also to pray that God gives them Godly spouses one day.

However, for me, as my mother's illness progressed, the tables turned. It was then my time to pray, light candles and vigil lamps, and pray more than ever, for my mother. I remember the day I was faced with the news that Mama could no longer swallow. I was having a hard time accepting not being able to do anything to help her, other than provide a little liquid to moisten her mouth. I felt anxious and stressed. I was trying to remain calm and trust God. In those last few days, I was comforted by this prayer I offered for my mother:

> O Most-pure Lady Theotokos, behold the victory of Truth in this, my Mama Danica's lifetime on the earth; make her worthy to be a partaker of the Blessed Joy before the hour of her death; so that she may together with the Angels and the Prophets, the Apostles, and all the Saints praise thy marvelous mercy and ascribe glory, honor and worship to the Holy Trinity, Father, Son and Holy Spirit, now and ever, and unto the ages of ages, Amen.

CHAPTER THREE

As time marched on, my strength departed and worry seeped in. I tried to focus on this shorter prayer instead:

Most Holy Mother of God, Save and Protect my mother!

As I prayed, I needed my Heavenly Mother to console me. I kept a small copy of The Pochaev Icon of the Mother of God in my hand for solace, and felt the grace of God whenever I did so. As my Mama began to slip away, I wondered if I had prayed enough for her soul. As fear washed over me, I kept thinking about so many different things it was hard to focus. So, I decided that I would think less and kept asking the Theotokos to intercede for me in prayer, to entreat Christ to save my Mama's soul, and to give me strength and peace.

It was heartbreaking each day to look at my skinny and frail ninety-year-old mother. It was painful to see her tiny body wasting away. But when I examined her face up close, she looked amazingly peaceful. She did not look upset at all. I was the one who was upset. I needed *her* peace. Mama's face looked like she trusted God. He had her in His Almighty hands. It was my faith that was lacking.

Then I thought about one of the Mother of God's most comforting references, "The Staff of Old Age." I remembered a beautiful hymn from the beloved feast of the Pokrov or Protection of the Mother of God. Amongst Slavic people, it is one of the most beloved feast days on the Orthodox calendar. Sometimes it is referred to as the Protecting Veil or Intercession of the Theotokos. This comforting hymn reminds me that whatever worries I had concerning Mama's impending death, The Mother of God had Mama *covered with Her prayers*. I felt such peace knowing this. The Theotokos truly was "The Staff of Old Age," praying for my beloved mother Danica. The following hymn says it all.

Kontakion (Tone 3)

Today the Virgin stands in the Midst of the Church And with the choirs of Saints She invisibly prays to God for us.

Angels and Bishops worship,

Apostles and prophets rejoice together,

Since for our sake She prays to the pre-eternal God.

I felt comforted by the intercessory prayers of the Theotokos. I cried out to her to come and help me and my mother, and to have compassion on us. I knew She had our backs. Her holy life keeps reminding me to yield to God's will without questioning. *All I could do then, and all I can do now, is pray. It is all we can ever do.*

As we head back to our discussion of The Pochaev Icon, it is important for us to remember that Orthodox icons portraying the Mother of God as the main subject are considered authentic and revealed truth, just like icons of Jesus Christ.

CHAPTER THREE

While some of the compositional elements in this particular icon of the Mother of God are unique to this specific prototype, others are true for all icons in general. It is important to understand each one.

There are several types of compositions or *icon prototypes* repeated in the icon tradition, each of which is created with specific motifs. For example, if we study an icon of Christ as the main subject, we might encounter a particular type of icon prototype called, *"Christ Pantocrator:"* Christ, the Ruler of the All. In this type of icon composition, you will see Christ portrayed frontally as a half figure with gentle eyes looking directly at the viewer. He wears a red tunic and blue cape which symbolizes the two natures of Christ. The band over his right shoulder harkens from the Roman imperial court which indicates a high official status. His right hand is raised in blessing. His left hand holds the Gospel. Everything in the icon supports the message of Christ as Pantocrator. This particular type of composition presents us with the striking image of All-ruler, Creator, Saviour and Judge of the world.

There are also many different compositional versions of the Mother of God in the icon tradition. One of the most famous prototypes is called *"Hodegetria"* (see example on page 82). Hodegetria is a Greek term meaning Directress. In this composition we see the Theotokos with Her hand raised, by which *She points us to Her Son*. Both are represented full face and turned towards the viewer. Christ sits upright supported by Her arm. His right hand is raised in a blessing and His left hand holds a scroll. On the arm of the Mother of

CHAPTER THREE

Christ Pantocrator Icon Prototype.

CHAPTER THREE

The Mother of God Hodegetria Icon Prototype.

CHAPTER THREE

God we see the majesty of Heaven enthroned. She presents the coming Saviour to the world. In this composition, we see the Mother of God showing us clearly *Who it is we need to follow.* It's interesting to note that we rarely see icons of the Mother of God without Christ.

The Pochaev Icon of the Mother of God represents yet another specific prototype in the icon tradition. This particular compositional version happens to be my favorite. Its spiritual beauty pulls at my heart. It is referred to as *"Eleousa,"* which means merciful in Greek. In Russian the word for this variant is *umilenie*. This translation is similar. The overall feeling this type of icon conveys is tender, mild, loving, and compassionate. There is more emotion presented to us in the Mother of God Eleousa variant and less formality than the last two icon prototypes. We see the mutual gestures of loving kindness between the Theotokos and Her Son. We feel a warmth and tenderness. The humanity of Christ and the compassion of the Theotokos are expressed. The Eleousa icon prototype we encounter in The Pochaev Icon depicts the motherly compassion the Theotokos has for all human beings.

I am one of those human beings the Theotokos has motherly compassion for *and so are you*. My mother reposed on June 28, 2022. She passed away right after I wrote the previous paragraph and inserted a photo of The Pochaev Icon immediately following it. I did not write another word for the next six months. When I returned to writing again after Mama's death, The Pochaev Icon of the Mother of God was the first image I saw. Talk

CHAPTER THREE

The Jordanville Icon of The Pochaev Mother of God represents the loving and compassionate Eleousa Icon Prototype.

CHAPTER THREE

about Divine timing, I felt my Heavenly Mother consoling me through this holy image. I could not write for several minutes, I kept looking at the icon. Her love drew me in. My eyes met up with Her compassionate and tender face as She held Her Son, my Lord and Saviour. I felt Her love and compassion not just for me but for all humankind. I thought about how She saw Her Son suffer and die. She understands human grief and pain. As our Heavenly Mother, She loves each one of us. She is our blessed refuge in times of hardship. I am so grateful the Theotokos is forever working to keep us on the true path to Christ. She is the *boundless sea of love* that keeps us sailing towards Him.

In the introduction of this book, I mentioned my hope and prayer that each of you will visit the holy and beautiful Pochaev Icon of the Mother of God, in the Saint Job Chapel in Jordanville. There, you will see the jewelry left behind with the icon as a physical witness to its miracles. However, it must be said, the major point here is not seeking miracles. The point instead is to seek *God*.

A visit to encounter The Pochaev Icon is about going to experience the holiness of a door that has been opened from the other side — the Heavenly Kingdom. When you stand before it and pray, you stand in the spot where other suffering people have also stood. The icon is the point where believers and God meet. We don't need to come just for a miracle, but we *should* come because *God is our only refuge*. In fact, we are instructed to do so: **"Come to Me, all you who are weary and burdened, and I will give you rest" (Matt 11:28, KJV).**

CHAPTER THREE

It has been a great balm for my soul to visit The Pochaev Icon of the Mother of God at Jordanville. I truly believe it was through the prayers of the Mother of God that I was able to go. This holy pilgrimage, first taken with my friend, and then again with my family, strengthened my faith and even prompted me to write this book. Furthermore, when I got home the spiritual rewards I received from my pilgrimage increased as I reflected upon my trip.

I received this spiritual sustenance I needed in order to endure the final — and most difficult — years of caring for my beloved mother. When, after over a decade of caregiving, I was weary and at my literal breaking point, the Theotokos stepped through the open door of my heart as I encountered the spiritual beauty of Her Pochaev Icon. Our Heavenly Mother tenderly reminded me once again to seek refuge in Her Son, my God. After my encounter, I could keep going because I knew God was right there at my side.

As an ethnic Serb, I grew up respecting and loving the Mother of God, who Serbs loving call *Bogarodica*. However, I never truly understood why She was considered such a powerful intercessor for us. This changed when my caregiving journey with my earthly mother opened my spiritual eyes. We can go to Church, read about Her in the Gospel or have icons of Her and Christ, but sometimes a personally meaningful experience is what moves our hearts to a deeper understanding of the person of the Theotokos. It is as if I saw a brief glimpse of Her spiritual magnificence through The Pochaev Icon. It's hard to explain in words. I just saw it and knew.

CHAPTER THREE

The icon expresses the great love and reverence She has for Her Son and God. She holds Him with such tenderness. She knows full well Who He is! What's even better is that She want us *all* to know Him. She cries for us when we don't. She constantly steers us back, again and again, on the True Path through Her powerful intercessory prayers. Our beloved Theotokos is truly the hope and consolation of the world. We need Her prayers. She is an unfathomable well of mercy for all Christians who honor Her.

Even outside of Church services, we can strive to draw near to Her. Call upon Her. Pray Her Akathist. I have recently found a park bench where I sit for a few minutes in the middle of my morning walk with my dog. This is where I share what's new with me, or what's got me stressed. There, I ask for Her intercessory prayers for my family and myself. This way I start my day with my Heavenly Mother but also my greatest friend in Christ. I am counting on Her ardent and intercessory prayers for me and my loved ones. She is devoted to keeping all of us on the True Path which leads straight into the arms of Her Son, our God. *I have no doubt, the Theotokos has brought me closer to Christ.*

My beautiful Serbian-born mother, Danica, has fallen asleep in the Lord. However, I am not left alone. My Heavenly Mother loves me and is forever with me. In fact, a few years before Mama's repose, I repeatedly asked the Theotokos to please ask the Lord to pick a special day for Mama to pass. I asked for a special and holy day. One that would have meaning for Mama and me. A day I would never forget. And indeed, my prayer was answered.

CHAPTER THREE

Our great Lord God gave me a beautiful and perfect consolation on the day and date Mama reposed, when He chose one of the most significant and unforgettable dates in Serbian Orthodox spiritual history. Ask any Serb! Mama died on the exact day, (Tuesday) and date (June 28th) of a major Serbian Orthodox feast day, Vidovdan or Saint Vitus Day. Vidovdan marks the day of the Battle of Kosovo, Tuesday, June 28, 1389.

Saint Barsanuphius of Optina (1845-1913) teaches us that our whole life is a great mystery of God. All of life's circumstances, no matter how insignificant they seem, have enormous meaning. There is nothing accidental in life; all is done according to the will of the Creator. The Saint also says we will understand the meaning of the present life in the future age. I find great comfort in the words of Saint Barsanuphius and think of them quite often.

The date Mama died (Tuesday, June 28th) represents an important turning point in Serbian Orthodox spiritual history. The meaning of Vidovdan is significant for any believer — Serb or not. On that day June 28, 1389 (which fell on a Tuesday), the Serbian leader and future Saint, Tsar Lazar realized he was significantly outnumbered in fighting off the Ottoman Turks as they were coming into his territory to conquer and expand their Muslim empire. The night before the battle, Tsar Lazar had a dream of a divine visitation from an angel. The Orthodox Christian Tsar was offered a choice between the earthly and Heavenly Kingdoms in the dream. Tsar Lazar chose the

CHAPTER THREE

Danica Velibor Dobrić Trifunovic
January 31, 1932 – June 28, 2022
Vidovdan (Saint Vitus) Feast Day is the day Mama
reposed in the Lord.

CHAPTER THREE

Eternal Heavenly Kingdom because he knew that choice lasts forever.

Before what became the Battle of Kosovo, Tsar Lazar and his troops celebrated Liturgy and took communion for the "*Honorable Cross and Golden Freedom.*" That day, or *Vidovdan* as Serbs know it, was seen as a spiritual battlefield. On June 28th the armies met on the Field of Blackbirds. There were heavy losses on both sides, but ultimately the Ottomans won. However, Tsar Lazar made the right choice. He chose to die as a follower of Christ.

He became a Saint and a great role model for Serbian Orthodox people. Through him, Serbian people learned to accept self-sacrifice and death as the triumph of *Truth in Christ*. This Serbian leader made the right choice. Tsar Lazar died for Christ and became a Martyr. The Battle of Kosovo continues to this day to represent the Orthodox Ethos of Holy Serbia.

Through his sacrifice, the great Martyr Tsar Lazar built the Church. When you look at an icon of Saint Tsar Lazar, you cannot help thinking about the story behind the icon. The Saints and their life stories show us the way to Christ. This is why they are preserved from generation to generation. As my mother always used to say, the Truth (with a capital T) always rises to the top.

God gave me this parting gift of my mother's special death date. I will never forget it. This special day will always remind me not to immerse my soul in the earthly kingdom. The day my mother reposed will stay etched in my heart. It will forever

CHAPTER THREE

remind me to choose the Heavenly Kingdom — as my Serbian Orthodox ancestors did.

I will never forget the meaning behind Vidovdan, June 28, the Battle of Kosovo. Saint Barsanuphius reminds me the date of my mother's death was chosen by God. It is a spiritual gift that I receive with a grateful heart. We must forever keep our eyes fixed on the Heavenly Kingdom. The holy icons of the Church exist to help us from becoming blind to Christ.

The Pochaev Icon, like all holy images in Orthodoxy, has powerful spiritual stories behind it. We must learn these stories to fully absorb and comprehend the spiritual beauty of the icon. Every part of these holy images exists to inspire us to strive to make the *right* choice. Day after day, the presence of the holy icon reminds us not to get too comfortable with our worldly lives. After all, spiritual battles are still being fought today.

For example, whenever I see an icon of Saint Tsar Lazar, his God-loving life reminds me of what it means to have the mindset of a martyr. Saint Tsar Lazar's faith in Jesus Christ made him choose the path of self-sacrifice.

Jesus Christ said, **"...whosoever will lose his life for my sake shall find it." (Matthew 16:25, KJV)** Saint Tsar Lazar's holy story of martyrdom now becomes an important part of our encounter with his Orthodox icon. The special day Mama died proves the point time and again that God is in charge of every single detail of our lives. This includes our names and important dates in life. *There are no accidents in God.*

CHAPTER THREE

Serbian Spiritual Hero, Saint Tsar Lazar

CHAPTER THREE

We have briefly reflected upon the significance of the main subject of the Pochaev Icon, the Theotokos. May we *always* remember, honor, and call upon the Mother of God. She is our Irreplaceable Helper in life. Now it's time to continue to elevate ourselves to the Heavenly Kingdom where truth, holiness, and goodness eternally shine. I hope your personal prayer life has been refreshed by contemplating the glorious spiritual magnificence of the Theotokos. In the next chapter, we will learn the venerable history and spiritual story behind The Pochaev Icon of the Mother of God.

Most Holy Mother of God Save and Protect us!
Memory Eternal, Mama!
Vjecnaja Pamjat Mama!

Ariane and her mother, Danica, in 1981
Volim tebe! (Love you in Serbian)

CHAPTER THREE

After her mother passed away, the author took this small Pochaev icon with her on a getaway trip to South Carolina.

CHAPTER FOUR

REJOICE, O PRAISE OF POCHAEV, THE HOPE AND CONSOLATION OF THE WORLD.

PERSISTENT PRAYER AND THE POCHAEV ICON STORY

CHAPTER FOUR

PERSISTENT PRAYER AND THE POCHAEV ICON STORY

P rayer is what got me through all those years of caring for my mother. Without it, I think I would have cracked.

Shortly after Mama's death, my husband surprised me with a relaxing and memorable mother-and-daughter getaway trip to my mother's favorite beach, near Charleston, South Carolina. I made sure to pack my tiny Pochaev Icon in my backpack. When we arrived, I placed it on my hotel room night stand, where it was a tangible reminder of God-given peace during the trip. I slowly began to exhale, after all those years of caregiving. I also reflected upon my life during the previous eleven years, during which I cared for her. As I did, I could not help but worry what my next cross would be. Thankfully though, I did not dwell on that thought. I was able to let go and enjoy the trip. Gratitude entered my heart.

CHAPTER FOUR

Psalm 135:1-26
(Orthodox Study Bible)

The author began to sing parts of it after her mother's repose.

Give thanks to the Lord, for He is good,
   For His mercy endures forever;
Give thanks to the God of gods,
   For His mercy endures forever;
Give thanks to the Lord of lords,
   For His mercy endures forever;
To Him who alone does great wonders
   For His mercy endures forever;
To Him who made the heavens with understanding,
   For His mercy endures forever;
To Him who made firm the earth on the waters,
   For His mercy endures forever;
To Him who alone made the great lights,
   For His mercy endures forever,
The moon and stars for authority over the night,
   For His mercy endures forever;
To Him who struck down Egypt with their firstborn,
   For His mercy endures forever;
To Him who led Israel out of their midst,
   For His mercy endures forever,
With a strong hand and an upraised arm,
   For His mercy endures forever;
To Him who divided the Red Sea into parts,
   For His mercy endures forever,
And led Israel through the midst of it,
   For His mercy endures forever,

CHAPTER FOUR

And who overthrew Pharaoh and all his host in the Red Sea,
   For His mercy endures forever;
To Him who led His people through the wilderness,
   For His mercy endures forever;
To Him who drew water from the hard rock,
   For His mercy endures forever;
To Him who struck down great kings,
   For His mercy endures forever,
And killed mighty kings,
   For His mercy endures forever,
Sihon king of the Amorites,
   For His mercy endures forever,
And Og king of Bashan,
   For His mercy endures forever,
And who gave their land as an inheritance,
   For His mercy endures forever,
An inheritance for Israel His servant,
   For His mercy endures forever.
For in our humiliation the Lord remembered us,
   For His mercy endures forever;
And He redeemed us from our enemies,
   For His mercy endures forever;
Who gave food to all flesh, For His mercy endures forever.
Give thanks to the God of heaven,
   For His mercy endures forever;
Give thanks to the Lord of lords,
   For His mercy endures forever.
                    — used with permission of
      St. Athanasius Academy of Orthodox Theology

CHAPTER FOUR

My overall feeling on that lovely adventure with my daughter was carefree and joyful. Sometimes I silently whispered to my mother, "Mama, we did it, we made it through, with God's help!" In my mind's eye, I imagined her responding, smiling and saying her famous congratulatory phrase: "Yes, we did — and with flying colors, Ariane!" During this trip, my daughter and I did lots of things to remember Mama. She loved poppies, so one day we painted a poppy flower next to her name on a beach-side pavement. A lady walked by and saw us doing this. She stopped and asked us what we were painting. After we told her, she asked us what day Mama died. I responded June 28, 2022. She grinned and said her birthday was June 28! This made us smile, so we asked her to take our picture.

After the painting project, we ate at a local beach-side restaurant. To our delight the server was Serbian. When we finished our meal, she surprised us and took care of our bill. One sunset we walked on the beach together and found two white roses in the sand directly in front of our bare feet. Lots of wonderful surprises like that happened on our special trip. The grace of God was following us.

Throughout the trip, I kept sensing an overwhelming feeling of thankfulness. It hit me at unexpected moments. Once I felt it in the ocean enjoying the waves while my daughter sat tanning on the beach. Out of the blue, I began to sing in gratefulness to the Lord after my mother passed away part of **Psalm 136 (KJV)** which is frequently heard in the Orthodox Church (see page 98). My heart began praying the words without any pre-

CHAPTER FOUR

planned thought. Suddenly the words burst out of me. And to my surprise, standing waist high in saltwater, I began to repeat a Byzantine chant and prayer: **"O give thanks unto the Lord for He is good; Alleluia. For His mercy endures forever. Alleluia."** The funny thing was I could not stop singing it out loud. Again, and again, chanting quite robustly, I knew I could be loud because no one could hear my voice. The sound of the waves crashing around me washed out my voice. It was a joyful release. This was my spontaneous prayer of thanks to the Lord for helping me endure my long-term cross with Mama. The prayer felt like a natural part of me. I couldn't stop smiling while I chanted. *It was like one big exhale.* Gratefulness to God poured out of me because I knew He had helped me endure to the very end.

As soon as we got home from this trip, I arranged for Serbian priest Father Marko Matić to officiate my mother's forty-day Memorial service at Saint Petka Serbian Orthodox Church in Nashville. I prepared the wheat for the memorial service and also a luncheon after church for people who attended.

Another beautiful miracle was given to me the morning of the memorial, when I dreamt of my reposed father smiling from ear to ear and looking directly at me. This dream made me happy. My mother had been a widow forty years prior to her death. My heart was filled with joy imagining them together again after so many years. My prayers for Mama continue, only now, I pray for her soul. After that, I had her six-month memorial. I love how the Orthodox Church

CHAPTER FOUR

instructs us to do this regularly for our departed loved ones.

All I can say is I am so glad God gave us eternal life. God-willing, I look forward to seeing my mother and father again one day. By His Resurrection, Christ opened the gates of the Heavenly Kingdom. Mama has now left her earthly cares behind. I, on the other hand, still have mine. I must persist in prayer and work on my salvation. I must also continue to pray for my mother and father. The Church teaches us that departed souls sense the prayers offered on their behalf and they are grateful for them. All I know is that when I pray for the souls of my parents, I feel spiritually close to them, so I continue in prayer in front of my icons. The older I get, the more prayers I seem to have for loved ones both living and reposed!

Sometimes I think about how much we have in common with a holy image like The Pochaev Icon. For example, a believer is called to pray without ceasing and an icon is created in prayer and *for* prayer. It is said that the breath of life in God is prayer. So, I guess one could also say, *there is no life without prayer to God.* Instead of focusing on the world *around* us, we must prayerfully cultivate the world *inside* us, which is the world of Christ. We strive to commune with the Heavenly Kingdom in every chapter of our earthly lives. This includes our happy and even sad chapters. Icons exist to help us *persist* in prayer so we become holy, like God. This way His image, like the icon, will be reflected in us. After all, you cannot hide true inner beauty. When Christ is inside us, everyone who looks at us will feel energized and peaceful.

CHAPTER FOUR

What I found spiritually uplifting about The Pochaev Icon was that the pilgrims who came to Jordanville were incredibly tenacious in their powerful prayers. Their hearts never gave up. At the end of their ropes, they stood before The Pochaev Icon of the Mother of God and obediently hung on to hope in The Righteous Judge. They knew their only hope is God. They waited for His will concerning their requests. They trusted Him and no other. The jewelry they left behind powerfully expresses two words: persistent prayer. We should all strive to commune with God and never cease to pray with the tenacity of these pilgrims.

One day my dear friend Elisa told me about a special parable she discovered in Luke (18:1-8). That verse tells the parable of the tenacious widow, which reminded Elisa of how she felt praying before The Pochaev Icon. The tenacious widow had no one to assist her with her needs. She was completely alone. She had no husband or son. Worse yet, she needed help to resolve an unjust situation she was facing alone. To top it off, she lived in a corrupt city with an equally corrupt judge — the worst of the worst — an unjust and God-less man. Nonetheless, she had a big problem and no one else to turn to except this judge. She felt taken advantage of and wanted justice against her adversary. So, over and over, she kept approaching the judge. Time and again she went to him for help. She never gave up. Finally, the uncaring judge could not take her pestering anymore. To get her off his back he granted her request and gave her justice.

CHAPTER FOUR

The tenacious widow's insistence and persistence reminded me of what I saw when I gazed upon The Pochaev Icon. Because of this parable I pondered the frequency and sincerity behind my prayers. It made me stop and think about how I pray. Then I began to reflect upon the ongoing prayers that clergy and pilgrims say before The Pochaev Icon. The widow reminded me of the pilgrims who come to Jordanville to pray there. They come again and again to visit. *They persist.* They stand before The Pochaev Icon with their problems and most of all, *they pray.* This parable teaches me something very important about how to pray. This widow shows us the value of being tenacious. Her continued efforts say: never give up on God. Keep trying to stay in touch with Him. Keep praying. You know the old saying: persistence pays off. If we persist with our whole being, our prayers can make a difference! Of course, in this parable, the judge is the complete opposite of God. But even this corrupt judge listened to this widow. We, on the other hand, have a just Judge who loves, cares, and provides for us. He knows and decides what's best for us. Imagine how He will hear and listen to our persistent prayers. When we trust Him, we are thankful for the prayer requests He does not answer as we *hope* He will. We should *always* have hope He will answer us with our best interests in mind.

Trusting God and persisting in prayer even when it's difficult is always the right road to take as we travel through life. Every chapter of our life stories must include prayer because nothing in life works without Him. When I first saw The Pochaev

CHAPTER FOUR

Icon, I felt something more than what I was seeing with my physical eyes. Now I understand more of the depth of what I felt when standing there. My soul was absorbing the entire story of this holy icon. I encountered those persistent, prayerful pilgrims through the jewelry left behind adorning the icon. I could relate to these pilgrims. I felt drawn to them. I understood their yearning for God because I, too, was enduring a cross. In a nutshell, *I was one of them.*

These Pochaev Icon pilgrims inspired me not only to persist in prayers I had given up on, but also to amplify my personal prayer life. One thing I started to do was to regularly pray the Akathist to The Pochaev Icon (available at the end of this book). If for some reason or another I am not able to say the whole Akathist prayer, I will make sure to say its concluding prayer whenever I can. I love this prayer. I feel meekness and tenderness when I read it. There is nothing better than humility and repentance to draw Christ into our hearts.

Here is part of it:

> O Most Holy Lady; we come in the profound humility of our heart, and we call upon thee: Remember not all our sins and transgressions, O Good One. But rather, stand before thy Son and God and stretch out thy Most-pure hands before Him and plead on our behalf, that all the sins we have committed be forgiven; that He turn not His Face away from us, His servants,

CHAPTER FOUR

> for all the failed promises that we have given; that He not take away from us His Grace, that leadeth all souls to salvation.
>
> Yea, O Lady, supplicate for us unto our salvation, and do not be dismayed by our lack of strength; but rather, look down and behold our groanings as we stand in prayer before thy Wonderworking Icon in our sorrow and our pain. Enlighten our minds with tender thoughts; strengthen Thou our faith; and allow us to taste the sweetest gifts of Love!

You will find the rest of this powerful prayer to the Most-Holy Theotokos at the end of this book. It is a beautiful way to start or end your day.

As time went on, the more I read, the more I began to understand the story behind the Icon. Above and beyond the pilgrims' jewelry and the beautiful outward appearance of the icon itself, this includes a spiritual battle and a venerable Saint. Everything I learned about the icon's history further strengthened my faith and trust in God.

An authentic Orthodox icon comes with a unique and important spiritual history attached to it. We too possess a unique and important life story sandwiched in between our birth and death. Throughout our lives, we are all called to commune with the Heavenly Kingdom and pray. It's easy to forget that we are also called to be dynamic icons reflecting the image of God within us. Icons remind us that all faithful

CHAPTER FOUR

believers are created as bearers of His image. Every icon presents us with its rich spiritual history as well as the wonderful ongoing opportunity to pray.

Oftentimes, however, we encounter a stumbling block. We cannot see the icon as a door to the Heavenly Kingdom. The icon becomes just another picture on the wall. This hindrance to seeing the truth of the icon is the illusion of the world. It's often difficult to let go of our worldly cares, to open our hearts to not only receive but also to understand what we are receiving. Most importantly, we cannot forget that the Heavenly Kingdom is always readily available for us. Whether in home or in church, oftentimes we forget to stop and venerate our icons. They come to life through our living prayer. When we are not in prayer, the door remains closed.

Some days we just cannot seem to shake off the world and its problems. They stick to us like glue. Our earthly cares weaken our faith, and we become spiritually blind. We no longer yearn for God. Our earthly cares make us insecure. Instead of lifting us up, we are brought down. Our spiritual strength dissipates into the earth.

As I sit down to begin another chapter in this book, I know the feeling. My doubt seeps in. I am no expert in anything. What makes me think I can write about The Pochaev Icon? How can I write about the truth that a believer with faith and hope can stand still before this icon and potentially encounter the Heavenly Kingdom? Can I prove the unprovable to my readers?

Thankfully, in my momentary doubt, I reflect once again upon my own Pochaev miracle. To this

CHAPTER FOUR

day, my dream journal entry from eleven years ago still surprises me. Once again, the entry was simply a few words I saw in a dream. They were: *The Pochaev Icon*. I had never even heard of the word Pochaev before this dream. Such an obscure word, I thought: *Pochaev? Does this word even exist* I wondered. I looked it up and it did. I was perplexed about what it could possibly mean. So, I documented this short dream in my journal and subsequently forgot all about it. Then, over a decade later, it was God's will for me to revisit my old journal entry.

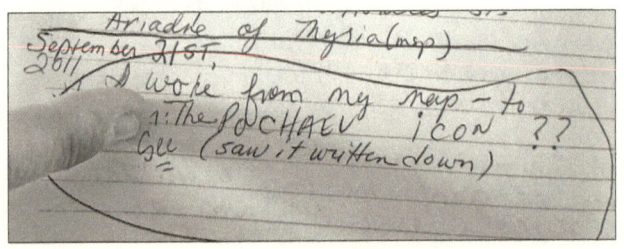

My very own Pochaev Icon miracle: my journal entry from September 21, 2011, which is one of the icon's commemoration dates.

When I re-found it, I had just returned from Holy Trinity Monastery where I had encountered this very icon. It was Divine Timing. I had written the introduction to the book and then, before starting my rough copy for Chapter One, right there in my journal, my very own Pochaev Icon miracle revealed itself. I had been looking for *other people's* miracles, and then I found my old journal entry with *my very own* miracle. How can anyone explain this? I cannot. I can only say, God is with us. God is with me.

CHAPTER FOUR

The author with her husband and daughter in Jordanville, holding their family's copy of The Pochaev Icon of the Mother of God.

This Heavenly remembrance and connection to a book I began writing eleven years after the dream still astounds me. My little miracle always lifts me up and gives me the spiritual courage I need to keep writing with God-given confidence. As I resume writing, I remind myself: God is with

CHAPTER FOUR

me at this very moment. I light my icon lamp and pray in front of my family icon of The Pochaev Mother of God. I whisper, *Mother of God, ask the Lord to help my unbelief.*

I love my family icon of The Pochaev Mother of God. I truly feel the Heavenly Kingdom when I pray before it. It hangs in my dining room on an eastern wall with an icon lamp in front of it. I now own a kiot (a protective glazed cabinet) for it to reside in, so that now, if I kiss my icon, the glass covering will protect it. My family icon is by Russian iconographer Elena Smirnova. I love her icons. She paints in a more western or academic style. Before it shipped, the icon was blessed in the

The author's family copy of The Pochaev Icon of the Mother of God, by Elena Smirnova. This icon prototype depicts Her footprint in the Pochaev Mountainside rock.

CHAPTER FOUR

Pokrova Mother of God Church in Cherkizovo, located just north of Moscow.

My icon has a slightly different composition than The Pochaev Icon I encountered at Jordanville. It has a footprint on the bottom of the image, and there are no additional Saints depicted on the sides of the icon. However, both versions are considered variants of the same Pochaev Iconographic prototype.

The Pochaev Icon of the Mother of God is one of the most sacred items of the Orthodox Church. Christians throughout the world venerate the icon, although it is especially renown in Slavic countries. No wonder Serbs like me love this icon! Truth be told, whether you have Slavic roots or not, it's important for every believer get to know this icon.

The original icon is now permanently housed in the Dormition Cathedral at the Pochaev Lavra (Monastery) of the Dormition of the Theotokos in Southwestern Rus', in Volhyn (now part of Ukraine's Ternopol Province). This is a location where borders between empires, civilizations, and world views clashed. According to several accounts, this holy monastery was founded by monks who fled from the historic Orthodox Kiev Pechersk Lavra (Kiev-Caves Monastery) which was founded in 1051 by a Greek Orthodox monk named Saint Anthony of Pechersk. The monks were forced to leave because of the of the devastating Tatar-Mongol invasion that fell upon Holy Rus'. The Pochaev Dormition Lavra is one of four great lavras in the Russian Empire. Around the end of the sixteenth century, it became an influential bastion of Orthodoxy. The monastery is

CHAPTER FOUR

The majestic Holy Dormition Pochaev Lavra (Monastery) crowns a sixty-meter hill in the town of Pochaev.

situated on a majestic cliff on the Volynia' upland, equidistant from Kiev and L'viv.

The Pochaev Icon is widely renowned for healing of the sick, deliverance from unclean spirits, and many other miracles. The Monastery keeps books with the signatures of the faithful who have experienced miracles associated with the icon. Throughout the centuries, a multitude of copies have been made of the original wonderworking image of the Most Holy Theotokos, such as the one I encountered at Jordanville. Many of these copies have also proved to be miraculous or wonderworking icons. The venerable and holy history of this icon connects these icons and their miracles. This is no surprise, because in God nothing happens by chance. This magnificent icon and its copies are inseparable links of one golden chain of holiness.

CHAPTER FOUR

The Pochaev Icon of the Mother of God is commemorated on the Friday of Bright Week, July 23/August 5, and September 8/21. There is no written documentation of the establishment and early history of the Pochaev Lavra (Monastery) located in the beautiful sub-Carpathian wilderness. However, local historical tradition tells us it was first settled around the end of the ninth century by several disciples of Saint Methodius (+AD 855) known as the Enlightener of the Slavs.

I remember my mother proudly telling me how successful Saint Methodius' missionary work was in Serbia. His disciples certainly went far and wide. Centuries later, during the Mongol invasion of Russia, two monks from the Kiev Caves Monastery settled in the area after the Mongols had sacked their city. The city was laid waste in 1240 by Baty (Khan). It is said that the monks named their new home after the river Pochaina, which flowed near the Kiev Caves.

Interestingly enough, my favorite Serbian Saint, Nikolai Velimirović, told the story of these two monks in his *Prologue of Ohrid*. In his book, Saint Nikolai tells us that in the province of Volinsk there stands a famous monastery of the Mother of God in Pochaev. She first appeared there around the year 1340 to two monks who were living the ascetic life in a cave. One of the stories about these monks is that one of them decided to climb up to the summit of Mount Pochaev to pray one evening. Suddenly, he beheld a pillar of fire burning in the wilderness. He quickly called out to the other monk to join him and continue in prayer as the fire glowed in the distance. Some shepherds who were tending flocks in the area also began to notice the fire. One of them named Ivan Bosoi ("the barefoot") joined the monks in prayer. As the three of them prayed, suddenly the fire opened before them. Surrounded by flames and standing on a rock, they beheld the Most Holy Theotokos.

When the flames withdrew and the vision eventually disappeared, they saw the place where they had seen Her standing had melted like wax. An imprint of Her right foot remained embedded in the mountainside rock. Over the footprint a fount of clear healing water also sprang up that same night. The previously uninhabited mountain become the holy site of a monastery dedicated to this miracle. This footprint with

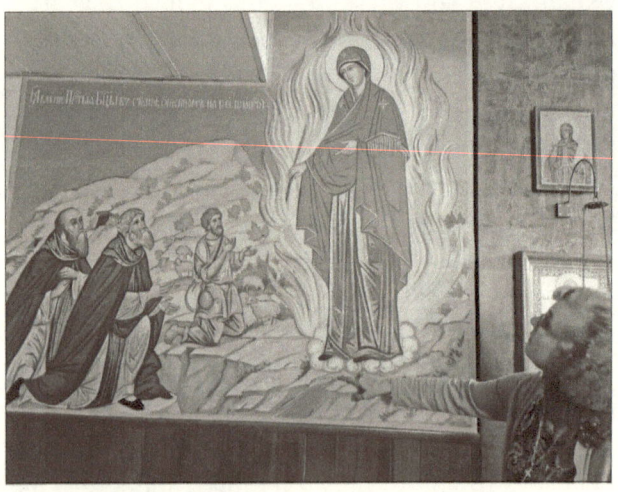

The author stands beside Jordanville's icon which depicts the miraculous appearance of the Theotokos on Pochaev Hill.

CHAPTER FOUR

the spring the Theotokos left behind still heals believers to this very day. My family icon depicts this miraculous footprint.

I truly marvel how God allowed this footprint to be left behind permanently. The footprint of the Theotokos leads us to Christ. Thankfully, we can still see it. God knows we need the physical witness of Her footprint. Lately, it's easy to become spiritually blind in this Godless world. We forget God, Our Creator. We may not be able to see Him, but the truth is He oversees everything there has ever been or will be. Theotokos' footprint makes me think of this verse:

Thy way is in the sea, and thy path in the great waters, and thy footprints are not known. Thy leadest thy people like a flock by the hand of Moses and Aaron. (Psalm 77 19-20, KJV)

This great miracle of supernatural phenomenon leads us to contemplate the venerable history of the original Pochaev Icon. The Most Pure One came in a pillar of fire standing above the Pochaev Hillside. What a marvel to imagine! Before I learned that, I thought only Mount Athos in Greece was the Mother of God's blessed and chosen place! The truth is that Pochaev has also long been a place chosen by the Mother of God.

After the devastating Mongol invasion and subsequent fall of Kiev, the legacy of the Kievan Rus' began to shift to the West. Because of this invasion the monks knew it was time to move. They

CHAPTER FOUR

eventually stopped at what would become Lavra Hill in Pochaev in 1240. To me, it is clear the Theotokos traveled with them during this difficult time. She instructed them to build Her monastery there, and thus the tradition of the Kiev Caves would continue in Pochaev.

The Theotokos instructed the monks to build Her monastery on Pochaev Hill.

In this venerable history, we see that God did not abandon these monks or the future generations of believers — like us. I believe He heard the ardent intercessory prayers of His Mother and chose to preserve the continuum of the True Faith. And, Glory be to God, just like that, the legacy of Holy Orthodoxy from Pochaev would be continued in Carpathia (central Europe). And then from Carpathia this holy legacy continued on to Jordanville, New York. Pilgrims like me who choose to visit Jordanville today can find the very same ancient Orthodox ethos in Holy Trinity

CHAPTER FOUR

Monastery, Seminary, its publications, its special copy of The Pochaev Icon of the Mother of God, and more. The holy legacy of Pochaev history is alive and well at Jordanville. One could say the Mother of God undoubtedly favors the continuance and remembrance of this venerable history. After all, She left physical evidence of Her footprint during Her visit to Pochaev.

It's a glorious sight to imagine. Right there in the rock, the solid limestone, the Theotokos stood in prayer. This footprint may be venerated in the Lavra's Holy Trinity Church. Pochaev is clearly under Her protection and later invaders would learn that Her power and might are unassailable. Soon, we too will see the enemies

Close up of Theotokos' footprint and fount of clear healing water, which is covered by glass at the Lavra's Holy Trinity Church.

of God fall before Her. They should never cross our unsleeping Mediatress. She is our defender *par excellence*.

CHAPTER FOUR

The Theotokos continues to this day to do so much for us by Her constant prayers. Through such prayers God allowed a miracle that has stood the test of time. He allowed the print of Her right foot to be left behind for us to see, as a visible reminder of our Ardent Intercessor. From generation to generation, we can profit spiritually by remembering this holy history. Her very footprint continues to be an ancient and holy treasure of Pochaev. Pure healing waters fill the footprint for us to freely partake of.

Just a couple of months ago when I went to Jordanville and spoke with Bishop Luke, he shared that he had actually visited the Theotokos' footprint and spring. What a blessing! As you can imagine, after witnessing this miraculous apparition the monks were forever changed. They got straight to work soon after this to glorify God.

At the base of the Pochaev Hill they built a stone church, in honor of the Dormition. Fast forward centuries later, the enormous Dormition Cathedral is now an even larger witness to this miracle. It was built in the Baroque style around the 1780s. The Cathedral encompasses the hill itself; the limestone footprint and sacred spring are all located on the very same site. The Cathedral rises dramatically high above the vast fields surrounding it. It is an imposing and unforgettable sight and the Pochaev Lavra (monastery and cathedral) can be seen from quite a distance. Sadly though, with the collapse of Rus' in the thirteenth century and the subsequent loss of its Southwestern lands, the monastery fell

CHAPTER FOUR

into decline. The good news is the monastery was eventually re-established at the turn of the sixteenth century.

In 1559, the Greek Metropolitan Neophit was traveling through the area. He decided to stop at the home of the pious and hospitable landowner, Anna Goiskaya. The Metropolitan was touched by her generous and warm hospitality. As a result, he left his kind hostess Anna a gift in gratitude. This gift was a special farewell blessing in the form of an icon of the Theotokos, which was painted in Constantinople. It was the original icon that would come to bear the monastery's name: The Pochaev Icon of the Mother of God. It is no wonder that the hostess was named Anna (which is Hebrew in origin) and means *God has favored me.* There are no accidents in God — even in the smallest details.

The next part of The Pochaev Icon story happened three decades later. The icon remained in the house chapel in the village of Urlya, not far from Pochaev. One night it began to emit a mystical radiance. People started noticing this. The radiance glowed like a warm fire. This was reminiscent of the fire 300 years earlier in which The Most Holy Theotokos appeared on Pochaev Hill. Right after this miraculous phenomenon, Anna's brother Philip — who had been blind from birth — gained his sight before the icon. Anna's family immediately took this as a God-given sign that the Mother of God's miraculous intercession came with a message. It was the Mother of God's intention for Her icon to reside in the restored Pochaev Monastery. In turn, the family faithfully

CHAPTER FOUR

The miraculous Pochaev Icon story is illustrated in this holy image. *We see The Pochaev Icon held reverently in the center of the composition with the monastery in the background. This holy image reminds us that Pochaev Hill is the Mother of God's chosen place as evidenced by the depiction of Her footprint, healing spring, and miraculous appearance in flames. We also see the four Venerable Pochaev Wonderworkers: Methodius, Job, Amphilochius, and Fedor Ostrozhsky gathered around The Pochaev Icon of the Mother of God.*

CHAPTER FOUR

gave the icon to the Pochaev Lavra along with many generous gifts to restore the monastery back to its former splendor.

Of course, the devil never sits still, as my mother used to say. So, after Anna's repose in 1644, all the surrounding lands were inherited by one of her family members. The sad reality was this family member hated the Orthodox faith. He decided to rob the monastery of The Pochaev Icon. However, God's will was for the icon to return. Almost immediately after taking the icon, the unjust man and his wife came down with a terrible sickness. They must have known their illness was connected to the removal of the icon, so they quickly returned the icon to its rightful place. As a result, they both recovered. We have a merciful and forgiving God.

Ever since the return of The Pochaev Icon, it has been housed in a bejeweled frame in the shape of a radiant star. The icon is located in the third row of the Dormition Cathedral iconostasis (a solid screen or wall of icons dividing the sanctuary from the nave in an Orthodox Church). Every so often, it is lowered down from its place to give pilgrims the chance to venerate it. The Pochaev Icon I encountered at Jordanville also has a beautiful star-shaped frame around it.

Mama's recent death has prompted me to notice anything that reminds me of her, so now stars catch my eye. The reason I have been noticing stars is because her name Danica means morning star. Danica is a popular Serbian name of ancient Slavic origin. Of course, you cannot but help to think of Jesus Christ when you hear the words:

CHAPTER FOUR

Morning Star. I love the words towards the end of **Revelation (22:16, KJV)** where Jesus Christ confirms exactly who He is, **"I am the Root and the offspring of David, the Bright and Morning Star."** Isn't it wonderful that even the frame of an icon leads you back to our Lord God and Savior Jesus Christ. May the grace of our Lord Jesus Christ be with all of us!

Every good and meaningful spiritual story usually has a battle and a hero. The spiritual hero (Saint) is the good guy and plays a significant role in the battle. And, it goes without saying, the battle is good against evil. In the next chapter, we are going to learn about a great battle and a great Saint connected to The Pochaev Icon. In fact, this Saint is one everyone should absolutely know. His name is Saint Job of Pochaev. What I've just described is an indelible part of The Pochaev Icon's venerable history. So, stay tuned, because more spiritual beauty will be revealed.

CHAPTER FOUR

*The Pochaev Icon of the Mother of God
is among the most venerable sacred items of
the Orthodox Church.
It is located in the Dormition Cathedral, Pochaev, Ukraine.*

CHAPTER FOUR

*The Copy of The Pochaev Icon
of the Mother of God at Jordanville.*

CHAPTER FIVE

REJOICE, O PRAISE OF POCHAEV, THE HOPE AND CONSOLATION OF THE WORLD.

HOLY HISTORY OF GRACE: A SPIRITUAL HERO AND BATTLE

CHAPTER FIVE

HOLY HISTORY OF GRACE: A SPIRITUAL HERO AND BATTLE

The grace of the Holy Spirit that accompanies a miracle-working icon offers every believer a refreshing breeze of spiritual nourishment. It's what our tired hearts need when our faith has become weak. Just one undeniable sign from God can be a great boost to our faith. Whether it's the original icon or a copy, this inherent God-given grace continues from generation to generation. Sometimes it's tangible — as seen in icons that stream myrrh (an aromatic oil). Or sometimes there have been self-restoring icons. These icons have been blackened with time and miraculously clean themselves to reveal their original vibrant colors. These types of miracle-working icons reflect a kind of grace that reveals itself in a form that you can see, smell, and touch.

CHAPTER FIVE

It's exciting to be in the presence of these types of icons. We all rejoice when God allows us to see an unmistakable miracle. The truth is miracle-working icons present us with certain unique spiritual revelations that go beyond the obvious. Each and every one of these icons reveals so much more than can be seen with our physical eyes. It is in our best interest to take time to get to know the history of these icons to receive the full spiritual gift they offer us. We must not let the miracle stop at what we see. The fullness of the miracle is revealed when we slowly unwrap our gift with time and thought. *After all, a miracle is not an end in itself.*

Our Almighty God is a mystery. But one thing is certain — we all long to have a stronger faith. A deeply personal experience with one of these icons encourages us in our spiritual lives, like my experience with The Pochaev Icon. Sometimes what is revealed is not for only one person. It's for the greater body of Christ. It might even be a spiritual message for the entire world. Perhaps this type of revelation could be understood as an intercession or maybe even a warning. Only God knows. Either way, the bottom line is everything these icons impart to us is a testament to our Almighty God's great mercy and love for His people. That's why the holy history surrounding these icons is also important to uncover and understand. This history is part of the miraculous gift we receive from God. This gift specifically includes historic people and events attached to the icon.

I will never forget the very first time I went to Jordanville. I had not yet had my encounter with

CHAPTER FIVE

The Pochaev Icon. Before that, I had the great honor of stopping and attending a Panikhida (memorial service) at the grave of martyr Brother Joseph Muñoz-Cortes.

The Lord chose him to be part of the holy ministry of a miracle-working icon of the Theotokos. I learned he was the devoted and righteous guardian of the Montreal Myrrh-Streaming Iveron Icon of the Mother of God. Many of you already know about this miraculous icon and its copy. It was a great tragedy: the icon disappeared in 1997 at the same time as the brutal murder of its devoted guardian.

Thanks be to God, there now exists an exact copy of the Montreal Myrrh-Streaming Iveron Icon of the Theotokos. It is called the Hawaiian-Iveron Icon of the Mother of God. This replica streams floral-smelling myrrh. As we learn more about this new icon, we see God shaping another spiritual hero. Father Nectarios Yangson has been charged by the Russian Orthodox Church with guarding, caring for, and sharing this myrrh-gushing icon with believers.

I recently learned of a story connected to the holy history of the Montreal Iveron Icon's guardian. It specifically relates to Brother Joseph's final days. Perhaps it is spiritual warning revealed. It is not as common as some other stories you might hear surrounding this icon. The story involves Brother Joseph and another miracle-working icon of the Mother of God he encountered in Greece. Shortly before his death, he visited a small Greek Orthodox Monastery dedicated to Saint Nicholas

CHAPTER FIVE

Brother Joseph Muñoz-Cortes, the Guardian of the Montreal Myrrh-Streaming Iveron Icon of the Mother of God.

CHAPTER FIVE

the Wonderworker, Archbishop of Myra. This ninth century Monastery is located on the island of Andros. It also housed a Myrrh-Streaming Icon of the Mother of God, which had been exuding myrrh for close to twenty years.

When Brother Joseph arrived in October 1997, the monks at the Monastery Church hastened to greet him. They were very excited to see him. They could not wait to tell him that their resident icon was weeping. One monk exclaimed, "The Mother of God has been crying." At first, Brother Joseph thought these monks were simply describing the phenomenon of myrrh-streaming. But one of them quickly clarified that The Mother of God was indeed crying this time. Tears were visible directly streaming from Her eyes. Brother Joseph bowed down and kissed the icon with great love. Then the monk continued his story in further detail. He said that the icon only weeps when something terrible had already happened *or was about to happen*. Brother Joseph was deeply moved. He stated shortly thereafter that he thought nothing was accidental about this miraculous weeping occurrence during his visit. He believed this phenomenon was a warning. Brother Joseph later confided to his travel companion that he felt something terrible was about to happen that involved him.

And something terrible did happen. Brother Joseph was brutally tortured and subsequently murdered shortly thereafter. His divinely ordained icon ministry abruptly came to an end. It was sealed with his martyr's death. In addition, the miracle-working icon mysteriously disappeared. It is said

CHAPTER FIVE

The back side of the memorial over the grave of Brother Joseph in Jordanville.

CHAPTER FIVE

Brother Joseph's body showed no sign of corruption or odor for almost two weeks.

People at Brother Joseph's funeral saw a transfigured expression. His face bore witness to the fact that he knew his suffering was ending and momentarily he would meet God. His face in death shows us the victory of Christ over dark forces. I firmly believe Brother Joseph's glory and honor will only grow like the special icon he guarded and took to all parts of the world. Many believe he will become a Saint one day. Only God knows.

Now through God's grace we have an exact replica of this missing Montreal Iveron Icon. It is called the Hawaiian-Iveron Icon of the Mother of God. Whenever I think of this present-day Hawaiian copy of the Montreal variant of this icon, I cannot help but reflect up the holy life of Brother Joseph. He has become an indelible part of the miraculous spiritual history of the original icon and its replica. To fully understand and appreciate this Orthodox miracle-working icon, we must also strive to learn about Brother Joseph, who dedicated his entire life to the service of the Theotokos.

Brother Joseph wanted to become an Orthodox monk. Unfortunately, during this time it was not possible since he lived in Canada, where there was no Orthodox Monastery. He knew he wanted to serve God but needed some direction. Not knowing what to do, he turned this request over to the Mother of God. The way he prayed to Her with such devotion is inspirational. He absolutely knew that the Theotokos is the constant advocate for us mortals. Brother Joseph reminds us that the

CHAPTER FIVE

Mother of God presents our entreaties before the King of Heaven. This martyr inspires me to strive to remember the Theotokos in my personal prayer life.

Brother Joseph's prayers to the Theotokos were answered. She heard his entreaties and presented them to the Lord. God allowed Brother Joseph the great and holy responsibility to be close to Her miracle-working icon. He was granted a holy role in life. He became the guardian of an icon that helped people find hope in their lives. He guarded this icon with every breath of his being. No doubt he understood the deep spiritual significance of his divine work. Brother Joseph surely knew by guarding the icon he was living on the edge of two worlds: *the visible and the invisible.*

Brother Joseph was a constant witness to the spiritual healing of human souls. Can you imagine all the miracles he must have witnessed? He lovingly brought the gates of Heaven to everyday-people — people like you and me. He travelled far and wide to all parts of the world bringing the icon to the faithful by visiting numerous parishes, churches, and monasteries. He worked diligently sowing Christ's vineyard. Think about how much the enemy of Christ's Church must have absolutely hated him. His terrible murder shows us the threat he was to satan.

The truth is he was an extraordinary spiritual hero. He was chosen by God. To this very day, Brother Joseph's life continues to be a beacon of light leading us to the Heavenly Kingdom. He was a selfless servant of God who worked with the Mother of God to bring people to Christ.

CHAPTER FIVE

Although it is hard to fathom his death, one thing is certain: he has now become part of the divine mystery of this icon. Even now, he leads us to Christ from his Heavenly abode. His life is permanently tied to the history of the miraculous icon he guarded. When we venerate the present day Hawaiian-Iveron replica, we also remember this unforgettable martyr. In him, God gave us a spiritual hero. We can see how the Mother of God reveals her mercies to mankind through the physical matter of the icon and also through the holy people connected to it.

Oftentimes, the spiritual heroes connected to certain miracle-working icons are Saints. For example, it's hard to think of the Kursk-Root Icon of the Mother of God "Of the Sign," without thinking of Saint Seraphim of Sarov. He was a venerable Russian ascetic who lived at the Sarov Monastery in the eighteenth century. He is considered a wonderworker in the Orthodox Church. At the age of ten he became seriously ill. During his illness he dreamt of the Mother of God, who promised to heal him. So, when the miracle-working Kursk-Root Icon passed his home in a religious procession, his mother took him up to venerate it. After this encounter, the boy quickly healed.

When you hear of a story like this, one thing is clear. You cannot separate the icon from its spiritual history. In fact, most believers would agree that you cannot think of this ancient Russian Kursk-Root icon without connecting it to Saint Seraphim of Sarov. The two are indelibly tied together. One cannot be separated from

CHAPTER FIVE

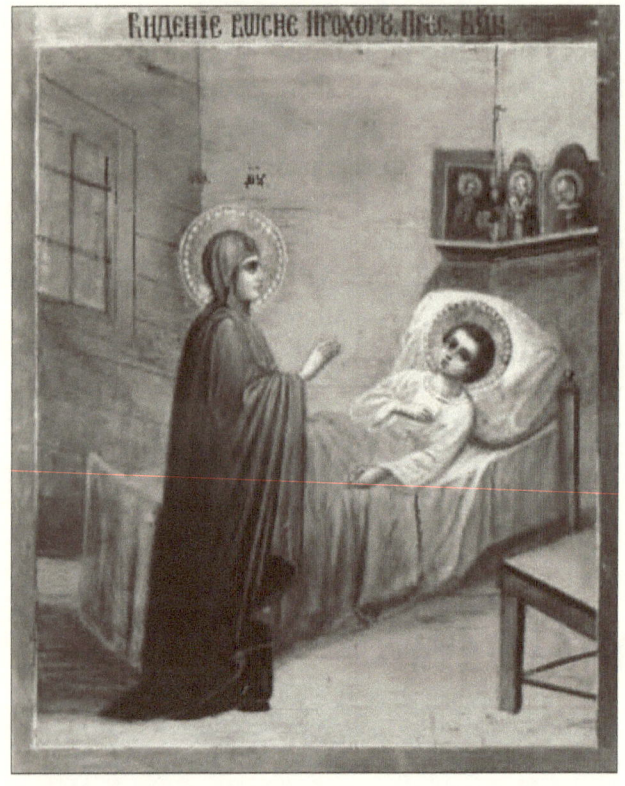

When he was a boy, Saint Seraphim of Sarov dreamed of the Mother of God, who promised to heal him.

the other. Both the icon and the Saint bestow incredible blessings to the believer.

A Saint like Saint Seraphim of Sarov and a martyr like Brother Joseph Muñoz-Cortes are part of the abundant grace we receive when we experience these miracle-working icons. The Pochaev Icon of the Mother of God also has a great spiritual hero attached to it. He is another one of the great Saints of the Russian Orthodox Church. His name is *Saint*

CHAPTER FIVE

Job of Pochaev, Abbot and Wonderworker of Pochaev. Perhaps this Saint is not as well known to the everyday Orthodox believer. I only learned of him because I visited Jordanville and wanted to know more about the history of its wonder-working icon: The Pochaev Icon of the Mother of God. However, Saint Job of Pochaev, one of the great missionaries of the Orthodox Church, should be known by all faithful. This righteous Saint is a Saint we need

After venerating The Wonderworking Kursk-Root Icon of the Mother of God, Saint Seraphim of Sarov was healed.

CHAPTER FIVE

especially now. He is a strong weapon we can call upon in the Godless times in which we live.

There is a complex holy history surrounding the Saint and The Pochaev Icon. The Icon and Saint Job of Pochaev are both connected to one of the most ancient domains of Christian Rus'. This area was referred to, in various sources, as either Volhyn or Volhynia. It was what Russian chronicles once called "Chervonnaya Rus'." The literal translation means Red Russia. This area was brought to the Orthodox Christian faith during the time of the holy and right-believing Grand Prince Vladimir, the Baptizer of Kievan Rus' (958-1015). It was ravaged by Mongol Hordes and occupied by Poland-Lithuania. Then it was absorbed back into the Russian Empire during the time of Catherine the Great. It also returned briefly to Poland after World War I. After World War II it became part of the Soviet Union. This area has suffered a history of unending tribulations. In fact, so many struggles befell this area that they are quite frankly too numerous to mention. However, with all that being said, to this day, it remains largely Orthodox.

At the heart of this turbulent region is the Holy Dormition Pochaev Lavra. This monastery had grown largely due to the efforts of Anna Goiskaya, a pious woman able to recognize the original wonder-working Pochaev Icon's holiness. It was she who knew this spiritual treasure must be shared, and it was due to her efforts that the icon came to reside in a holy place where it is venerated by other believers.

Saint Job of Pochaev holds the distinction of being one of the great Saints of the Russian

CHAPTER FIVE

Orthodox Church. He was also the very first abbot of the Pochaev Lavra. Even today, he is known as the pillar of Pochaev. His life remains as a testament to his indomitable faith. His was a faith that any true believer strives for. One section of the Akathist to Saint Job sums him up best. He is described as the "unconquerable defender and struggler of the Eastern-Orthodox catholic faith against the falsely minded West." Saint Job was a fearless preacher of the true Faith and strict upholder of the God-inherited rules of the Orthodox Church and its patristic inheritance. His venerable relics exist even today for veneration by each pious pilgrim. The Pochaev Icon of the Mother of God connects us all to this beautiful Saint. It's no wonder that Theotokos favored Saint Job because he was an ascetical, wise, and steadfast guardian of the Orthodox faith and its faithful.

Saint Job of Pochaev teaches us many soul-profiting things. One of his most important spiritual teachings is to show us how to never give in to change that corrupts our faith. Saint Job is the embodiment of what it means to hold steadfast. We must preserve our faith for future generations. He shows us we can all become missionaries for Orthodoxy within our families. We can use multimedia and books and podcasts and more to educate. This spiritual hero shows us the way! He brought the faith to the people, and we, too, must bring the faith to our families.

Bishop Luke of Jordanville was the first to help me understand exactly why Saint Job was such a great and tireless missionary. He explained that

CHAPTER FIVE

Saint Job of Pochaev (1551-1651), holding the priceless treasure of his monastery, the original miracle-working Pochaev Icon of the Mother of God.

CHAPTER FIVE

Saint Job was an ardent defender of the Orthodox faith. Bishop Luke continued by telling me that Saint Job established a printing press at Pochaev. Thereby, he was able to defend the faith in many different ways — including spiritual education through the written word.

His passion for preserving the faith is an inspiration for us all. Let's face it, we must be educated and know the treasure of the Orthodox faith we've been given. Just being born into it — like I was — is not enough. We need to know the basics of our Orthodox faith. We need to keep learning, and grow in the faith… not just grow old in it. This wise Saint knew spiritual education is powerful. Saint Job saw that it was the only way to preserve our faith for the future.

Before we discuss the details of Saint Job's life, it's important to understand a little about the complicated state of the world in which he was born. By doing so, we can understand why he continually struggled to defend the Orthodox faith throughout the course of his entire life. First, it's important to bear in mind Saint Job was born in the wake of the Protestant Reformation (1517-1648), just five years after Martin Luther's death (1483-1546). Luther was the Catholic monk who precipitated the Protestant Reformation by nailing a list of demands for reform on a church door. He had come to the realization that the Roman Church had become morally corrupt over time. The Latin Church responded to this by excommunicating Martin Luther in 1521 and eventually launching its own Catholic Counter-Reformation. Sometime

CHAPTER FIVE

Saint Job of Pochaev's printing legacy lives on at Jordanville through its Holy Trinity publications:
https://www.holytrinitypublications.com

CHAPTER FIVE

after this, the Catholic Church organized the Council of Trent to address internal issues and to vigorously combat the Protestants in response to their accusations of moral decay.

What's important to note from any of this history is how it directly affected Saint Job and his homeland. It must be said that before the time of the Protestant Reformation the Roman Church had not been aggressive towards the Orthodox in this area. However, all this all changed when the Catholic Counter-Reformation unleashed a new type of zeal. The side effect of this zeal directly affected Saint Job. The Roman Church suddenly began to take a renewed interest in the Orthodox Christians that lived in some of their Roman Catholic Kingdoms. They specifically targeted the Polish Kingdom which controlled most of the Ukraine. This began a time of troubles for the area. Saint Job grew up amidst the backdrop of this complex and difficult time for the Orthodox faithful. He constantly fought to defend his Orthodox flock from outside aggressors, some of whom were Roman Catholic and others, Protestant. This historic backdrop which unfolded around the Saint was a never-ending battle filled with power struggles and religious turmoil.

It was into this chaos that Saint Job of Pochaev was born around 1551 near Kolomyia in the Ruthenian Voivodeship of the Polish-Lithuanian Commonwealth (modern-day Ivano-Frankivsk, Ukraine). His family belonged to the class of Galician-Russian noblemen. Their most precious inheritance was Orthodoxy and a sense of belonging to the Russian nation. From his

CHAPTER FIVE

youth he modeled his life after Saints Sava, John of Damascus, and John Climacus. Saint Job's name before monasticism was Ivan (John, after Saint John the Baptist) Zhelezo. God gave him a name that would characterize his entire life and missionary work. It's incredible that his surname Zhelezo means iron, because he was strong like iron in his Orthodox faith. Iron has always been the go-to metal for tool and weapon makers throughout the ages, and Saint Job was a spiritual warrior. His Orthodox spirit was strong as iron. Nothing or no one could break him. Venerable Saint Job of Pochaev came to be known not only as strong but also steadfast and unwavering in his faith. No matter what tribulation was sent his way, he would not break. He just continued to pray and work through every struggle in life.

Before we get into the tribulations of his long (over-one-hundred-year) life, you cannot help but think of his monastic Old Testament namesake, Job, the Long-Suffering. Everything Job, the grandson of Abraham, had was taken from him. To most, his life looked like a losing battle. A no-win situation. All he had left in the end was patience and faith. With the weapon of faith and patience he overcame horrible satan. This Righteous Old Testament Job won. The same spiritual success followed Saint Job of Pochaev. His long-suffering tribulations bore fruit we witness to this day. Clearly God had picked the perfect monastic name of Job, for Ivan (John) Zhelezo.

The running theme of his life was a never-ending struggle. Thankfully though, he also possessed the

CHAPTER FIVE

weapons of faith and patience. Both Saint Job and his Old Testament predecessor knew God allowed their struggles for a reason. Let's face it: it's hard to accept a struggle you don't anticipate, but as Saint Anatoly of Optina once said, tribulations are the innermost grace of God. Saint Tikhon sums up this thought further by his words: "The absence of tribulations is a sign of abandonment by God." Time and again, I remind myself that the only reason I noticed The Pochaev Icon was because of the cross Mama and I bore together. It may sound odd to some, but we should always thank God for the tribulations he sends us. One day, we will be eternally grateful for them.

At age ten, Saint Job of Pochaev left his beloved and pious Orthodox parents, Ivan and Agafia, and arrived at the Transfiguration Ugornits Monastery in the Carpathian Mountains, and at age twelve he received monastic tonsure (small schema) with the name Job. It is said he became a true role model for the monastic life. Already in his youth, he was known for his great piety and strict asceticism. Around the year 1580, he was appointed head of the Exaltation of the Cross Monastery near the city of Dubno. He was the abbot of this monastery for more than twenty years, actively defending Orthodoxy against its enemies. During this time there was a growing persecution of Orthodoxy on the part of Uniates (Greek Catholics). The Uniates had left the Orthodox faith for the protection of the Roman pope. During this turbulent time the faithful turned to Saint Job for guidance. He stood unwavering in the Orthodox faith and with an iron

CHAPTER FIVE

will struggled against the Uniate threat. He used all his resources and unseen prayers to strengthen and protect the Orthodox faith and the faithful in the area.

He was a very spiritual man. His ascetic labors and pious life were hard to hide from the people around him. As a result, he became very popular, and his fame spread quickly throughout the entire region. One day he decided to flee the spotlight and glory of this world. In 1604, he secretly left for Pochaev Hill. He settled in a cave there, not far from the ancient Dormition Monastery, famed for its Pochaev Icon of the Mother of God. However, even there this holy hermit was eventually discovered. Once again, he became highly regarded for his strict monastic life. In time, he gave in to the monks insistent requests and was unanimously elected by the brethren as Abbot of Holy Dormition Pochaev Lavra. He faithfully fulfilled his duty as head of the monastery. It is said he was gentle and kind with all brethren. He worked hard at the monastery including physical labor from planting trees, plowing the fields, and even improving the monastery's water system. Under his leadership, the monastery became the greatest of the western Russian Monasteries. He also received significant support from local nobility. Because of this, in 1649 he was able to build a stone church dedicated to the Holy Trinity. This is where the imprint of the healing foot of the Mother of God, along with Her miracle-working Pochaev Icon reside.

Saint Job was a great defender of the faith. In 1596, another tribulation took shape. The Union

CHAPTER FIVE

of Brest was signed. The Union had both political and religious aspects. It was a devious plan to bring Orthodox subjects into the Latin Church of their Polish sovereigns. Many Orthodox living in Poland were deprived of their rights and were pressured to convert by accepting the authority of the pope, thereby breaking their union with the Orthodox Church. Saint Job fought against this threat through prayer and education. He realized the average Orthodox lay person needed to be educated to withstand this attack against the Orthodox faith. Many Orthodox people were tricked into converting. Even after submitting to change, many believed they were still Orthodox. They thought their Orthodox faith would remain the same with only a change in leadership under the Roman pope. The authorities in the area were continually forcing the Orthodox to submit to the pope. Those who would not accept this conversion were treated very harshly. The state of the church in this area was poor, clergy and laity were uneducated. This greatly troubled Saint Job. He used the printing press to fight back and became a great missionary and spiritual leader through the written word. He knew the only way to defend the Orthodox against the Uniate scheme was through prayer and the education of his flock.

He began to copy and disseminate Orthodox books. There was one Slavic printing press in Pochaev that he actively used to publish Orthodox prayers, teachings, and epistles. Saint Job witnessed the cruel ecclesiastical and political oppression from Polish-Lithuanian magnates as well as the growth of the Protestant influence. He used all of his influence

CHAPTER FIVE

to strengthen Orthodoxy not only through his visible labors but also his unseen labors of prayer. He also took part in the defense of Orthodoxy and the Russian people by attending the 1628 Kiev Council, which convened against the Unia. I remember seeing an icon of Saint Job holding a scroll. The scroll read as follows: Behold a sower went out to sow his seed and as he sowed, some fell on good ground and bore fruit a hundredfold. It's clear so much good fruit came from Saint Job's life of tribulations! He endured to the end with a steadfast will, always standing on Orthodox ground.

After 1642, he accepted the Great Schema. They say his heart was always occupied with unceasingly saying the Jesus prayer. Sometimes he would even conceal himself in a cave carved into the Pochaev cliffs for three days or even up to a whole week. He could neither sit or lie down comfortably in this cave. According to his disciple Dositheus, (author of the Life of Saint Job), once while he was praying in his cave, an extraordinary Heavenly light illumined the cave for about two hours. Saint Job truly became a temple for the living God. He reposed in the year 1651 after directing the Pochaev Monastery for more than fifty years. He was one hundred years old, and they say he died with a full set of teeth!

It's no wonder that people come from all over the world to venerate his holy relics. They can be found in a reliquary within the cave where he had piously prayed, on the Pochaev Hill. For the most part, the relics are covered with glass, although the hands of the incorrupt relics are uncovered. The faithful are given the opportunity to kiss

CHAPTER FIVE

Saint Job of Pochaev, Defender of the Holy Orthodox Faith.

CHAPTER FIVE

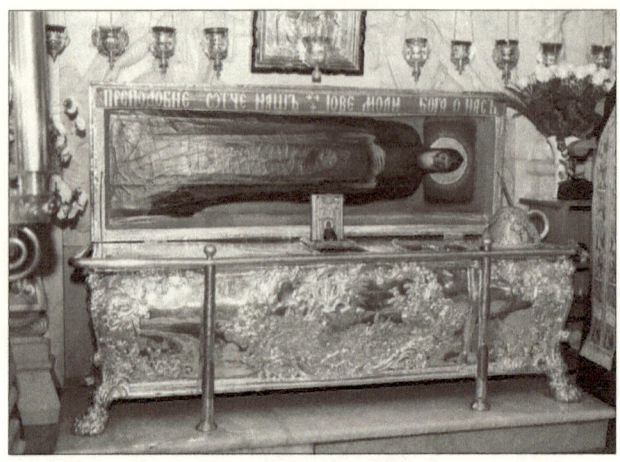

The relics of Saint Job of Pochaev were transferred to the Cathedral of the Life-giving Trinity on August 28, 1659.

them. Although he reposed many centuries ago, his hands are still soft and warm, and a beautiful fragrance exudes from them.

You can even climb through the Saint's tiny cave to pray there if you wish. It's a small opening in a cliff so you must go in headfirst and downward dive, so to speak. You enter a small space in total darkness. There is someone there to guide you to the icon so that you can venerate it. After this, you squeeze your way out of Saint Job's cave. But those who enter say they feel transformed when they return to the world. People speak of the awe that they feel after the visit; it's as if they had just seen the Face of the Lord.

Saint Job received a revelation about a week before he died that his end was near. He served Liturgy and then peacefully departed. He was buried near the cave where he prayed and practiced asceticism.

CHAPTER FIVE

They say a glowing radiance was often seen over his grave. Seven years passed and Saint Job came to Metropolitan Dionysius (Balaban) of Kiev three times in a dream. Saint Job told him it was time to uncover his relics. It was found that his relics were incorrupt and were filled with a wondrous fragrance. His feet had wounds from long-term swelling no doubt caused by long times standing in prayer. After this, his incorrupt relics were translated (the formal movement of holy objects) to the Church of the Life-Creating Trinity.

Many miracles have occurred from his relics. Even the Saint's biographer witnessed a personal miracle. He was fatally ill and was healed by Saint Job's prayers in 1659. At that time, Dositheus was the Abbot of the Pochaev Monastery. Just days after the uncovering of the relics of Saint Job, Dositheus became very sick and things went from bad to worse. Suddenly, one evening it was clear he had a life-threatening fever. Everyone at

Procession with the relics of Saint Job of Pochaev.

CHAPTER FIVE

the monastery caring for him gave up all hope for his recovery. The feast of the Elevation of the Cross was being celebrated during this difficult time. In addition, a benefactress of the Monastery, Lady Domashevskaya, had just arrived in Pochaev with her handmaiden, to pray and attend church services during this precarious time for the Abbot and his monastery. The benefactress must have felt the tension in the air that night.

Tired from her journey, she retired in her cell to rest. In the middle of the night, she woke up to beautiful chanting emanating from the church. She also saw a warm glow of light coming from the church windows. She sent out her handmaiden Anna to see what was happening. Anna went out and saw that the church doors were wide open. She entered and saw a bright light with Saint Job of Pochaev standing directly in the middle. He was praying between two shining youths with radiant garments. She immediately froze in fear. Then the Saint and the youths turned to her and said, "Fear not, maiden, but go and request that the abbot of this monastery come see me." Anna responded by saying this was not possible because he is dying. Then Saint Job gave her a silken handkerchief soaked with myrrh, and told her to give it to the sick man. So, she ran to the door of the abbot's cell and gave him the handkerchief. She told him in the name of the newly-revealed Saint Job of Pochaev to come immediately to the church.

At first Abbott Dositheus thought this woman's appearance was a dream. But then he saw the handkerchief was real and anointed himself with the

CHAPTER FIVE

myrrh all over his body. At once he felt completely well and whole. He then got up from his bed and went straight to church. However, by the time he got to church the Heavenly vision had ended. He knew he was healed through the prayers of the blessed Job! He then continued to stay in church to serve an all-night vigil giving thanks to God. All those seeing this were amazed. Just the night before he had been on his death bed. The abbot wrote that Saint Job had prayed with the angels to the Theotokos for his salvation. He even said the hands of the angels had opened the church doors. He was granted a magnificent miracle by the newly revealed Saint Job of Pochaev.

Some miracles can even fall under the category of righteous anger. Saint Job knows he is a Saint. This begs the question, what happens to people who do not respect Saints? Saint Job gives us the answer. Around 1711, a man named Lord Kaminsky came to the monastery with his two brothers. He asked the abbot to allow them to pray in the church. His doubting brother Vladislav secretly mocked the monks. He said he thought the monks dried out one of their elders and put him out on display to deceive people for money. After the brothers left and returned home, Lord Kaminsky was awakened by a scream in the middle of the night. It was his brother Vladislav who cried out in fear. He told his brother he had seen a terrible old man that frightened him. It was Saint Job of Pochaev who threatened him with his staff. The Saint asked Vladislav how dare he speak blasphemously of the Saints of God? Then he exclaimed, "Save me from

CHAPTER FIVE

the hand of blessed Job Zhelezo! The next day, all three brothers went back to the monastery. This time, they prayed for forgiveness and testified under oath to this miraculous occurrence, and it was recorded as a miracle. Venerable Job showed forth his power through righteous anger. This miracle is also a witness to his holiness.

Even after his repose, Venerable Job never forgot his monastery. One of the most incredible and memorable miracles to occur after Saint Job's death involved a battle launched by enemies of God against it. The good news is through Saint Job's prayers, the Mother of God saved the monastery from the Tatar and Turkish attacks in the summer of 1675. This was known as the Zbarazhsk War. Even though Pochaev had Cossack guards, it was very unlikely they would be able to survive any kind of protracted siege. The Monastery walls were not strong and therefore would not offer much defense against an attack. Because of this, the Turks were certain they would win.

The Turkish army made its way to the Pochaev mountain with the goal of expanding Islam. Father Joseph Dobromirsky was the presiding Abbot of the Monastery at this time. He quickly urged the brethren and laypeople to turn to their Heavenly intercessors. The faithful immediately began praying to the Mother of God and Saint Job of Pochaev. The monks and the laypeople stopped everything and prayed. They also begin to prostrate themselves before the wonderworking Pochaev Icon of the Mother of God, as well as the reliquary that contained the relics of the recently reposed Saint Job of Pochaev.

CHAPTER FIVE

The Righteous Saint Job of Pochaev.

CHAPTER FIVE

On the early morning of July 23, the Turks were getting ready to wrap up their win with one more assault. That morning the Abbot of the Monastery ordered everyone to sing the Akathist to the Mother of God. As people began to sing the first words, "To Thee the Champion Leader," suddenly a vision of the Theotokos appeared in the sky before everyone, radiating Divine Light and shining like a star. She stood in mid-air while commanding the Heavenly angels that appeared on either side of Her. The angels surrounding Her held unsheathed swords. Saint Job appeared beside her. Saint Job could clearly be seen bowing to the Mother of God and repeatedly imploring her to defend the Monastery. The Tatars took one look at the apparition and were terrified.

Saint Job, Kneeling Before The Mother of God And Imploring Her To Defend The Pochaev Monastery Against The Enemies of God.
The Monastery Was Miraculously Delivered from the 1675 Turkish Assault During The Zbarazh War.

CHAPTER FIVE

All the angels were there ready to defend the Pochaev Hill. The Queen of Heaven and Earth was leading the way in protecting Her chosen garden as well as fulfilling Saint Job's request. Each angel had flaming swords drawn. They were ready to defend. According to tradition, the Turks and Tatars went mad at the sublime and holy sight they saw before them. When they saw it, they were terrified and lost their senses. They started to shoot at the apparition. But the arrows changed course and flew back down upon those that shot them — like a boomerang. They either died on the spot, or in panic and confusion trampled each other. Some of the attackers were captured. What's even more amazing is that many prisoners came to believe in Christ after this incident. Some even became monks and remained at the monastery. As you might imagine, the faithful were overjoyed.

Pochaev was saved, the Monastery was saved, and the original Most Holy Mother of God Pochaev Icon was also saved. When the holy apparition disappeared, it left behind a bright evening star. Thanks to the prayers of Saint Job of Pochaev, this great fortress of Orthodoxy, the Pochaev Lavra was protected by the Queen of Heaven, the Theotokos. Who wouldn't want to get to know and commune with a powerful Saint like this?

After the sacred struggles of Saint Job, The Holy Dormition Pochaev Monastery received the status of a venerable Lavra. Even to this day, the Pochaev Lavra stands as a stronghold of Russian Orthodoxy amidst lands that have been ceaselessly subjected to Greek-Catholic invasions. The legacy

CHAPTER FIVE

of Saint Job reminds every believer to get to know our holy Orthodox faith in a deeper way. Once we understand its fullness, we would never be swayed to give it up under any circumstance. Every believer can be inspired by the steadfastness and holy iron will of Saint Job of Pochaev.

I am so grateful to the Lord God that I got to know The Pochaev Icon of the Mother of God and its history. Otherwise, I might never have encountered Saint Job of Pochaev. While getting to know this Saint, I have come to the realization that we need him now more than ever. We need to arm ourselves with this Saint in order to survive the tumultuous and Godless times in which we live. He faced so many challenges trying to preserve the Holy Orthodox Faith.

Saint Job's life reminds me of a Serbian book my mother gave me when I went off to college. The title of the book is *Orthodoxy: Courage to be Different — Strength to Remain the Same*. During his lifetime, Saint Job of Pochaev saw that many Orthodox believers did not know their faith or its history very well. They were lacking in knowledge, so they were ill-equipped to handle any threats to their faith. Back in Saint Job's time, this included both laypeople and some clergy who were uneducated. Neither could muster up the courage to remain the same. The truth is, this could easily happen to any Orthodox Christian. Saint Job of Pochaev fought all his life to teach his flock who they were as Orthodox believers. His mission continues to this day.

It does not matter how you become an Orthodox Christian. Like me, you can be given it on a silver

CHAPTER FIVE

platter by having Orthodox parents. Or you can discover it through much soul searching. Either way, with each passing year you come to the realization you've been given an incredible treasure by God. What is heard in Church on the first Sunday of Great Lent sums this up best. We hear the celebratory words of the Triumph of Orthodoxy and the victory over iconoclasm declaring what our faith truly is. This is read aloud from the Synodikon proudly announcing: "This is the Faith of the Apostles, this is the Faith of the Fathers, this is the Faith of the Orthodox, this is the Faith which has established the universe. This is our Orthodox Faith…" Then after this is read, the clergy and the people recite the Nicene Creed.

Saint Job taught his people all about the Orthodox Faith in every way he possibly could. He knew that if believers did not know their faith, they were in trouble. Every Orthodox Christian should know get to know Saint Job for this very reason. This way we can all become missionaries for the Faith, especially for our families. We can always do more to educate ourselves at home. Every dinner time when the family is together, at some point we can share a short story or quote from the lives of the Saints. Sometimes I read from the gospel or play a video pertaining to a feast day celebration. There are many ways to share our faith in little ways with lots of love! All these spontaneous little ways will add up, and we will be able to preserve our faith for our future generations.

All things done in sincere love are remembered. I love how Saint Job was gentle and kind. His biographer recorded these precious virtues. We are not going to win people over with aggression. Instead, like Saint Job, our weapons should be education, gentleness, and love. Saint Job had an iron will and was steadfast. He led with strength, knowledge, and kindness. Saint Job inspires us to be missionaries in our own families and beyond. We live in a world with many different theological confessions of faith. We must live in the world and not be changed by it.

Even as a religious minority in America, we must know exactly who we are as Orthodox Christians. We cannot give into outside influences just because everyone else is doing this or that. We can be okay with being different if we *know why we are different*. Christians were a minority in the Roman Empire, too. The early Christian Martyrs were different from their social environment. Saint Job can inspire us with the courage to be different and the strength to remain the same. Praying to Saint Job strengthens my faith. Oftentimes in moments of fear or worry, I think of the Saint when I need to be stronger in my faith. I simply pray: Holy Righteous Job, the Much-Suffering and Venerable Father Job, pray to God for me and help me become stronger in my faith!

Sometimes when I have more time, I light my lampada (icon lamp) and stand in front of my Pochaev Icon of the Mother of God to pray. It is during this time that I started praying to both to Saint Job and the Theotokos at the same time. The following is my favorite prayer which addresses both Saints in such a beautiful way. I feel this prayer sums up the spiritual beauty of Saint Job as well as the spiritual magnificence of the Mother of God. It is an excerpt from the prayer service from the little vespers honoring Saint Job of Pochaev (October 28).

Seminarian Nicholas Pavuk (on the left) at the celebration of the Feast Day of Saint Job of Pochaev (October 28) in Jordanville.

> Having found the most precious icon of the Mother of God on the mountain of Pochaev to be like the sun upon the earth, thou didst show thyself to be its most splendid star. Wherefore, through the supplications of the Theotokos, with the light of knowledge divinely illumine us who hymn thee, O Job, our father.
>
> *Glory…, Now and ever…, Theotokion, in the same tone —*
>
> On thee do I set mine every hope, O Mother of God. Keep me under thy protection.
>
> *Troparion, in Tone IV —*

CHAPTER FIVE

> Acquiring the patient endurance of the long-suffering forefather, emulating the abstinence of the Baptist, and sharing in the divine zeal of both, thou wast vouchsafed worthily to receive their names, and wast a fearless preacher of the true Faith. Wherefore, thou didst lead a multitude of monks to Christ, and didst confirm all the people in Orthodoxy. O Job our venerable father, pray thou that our souls be saved.
>
> *Glory…, Now and ever…,Theotokion —*
>
> The mystery hidden from before the ages and unknown even to the angels, through thee, O Theotokos, hath been revealed to those on earth: God incarnate in unconfused union, Who willingly accepted the Cross for our sake and, thereby raising up the first-formed man, hath saved our souls from death.

From the Liturgical Service honoring Saint Job of Pochaev, from the Life, Liturgical Service, and Akathist Hymn ,
St. John Of Kronstadt Press 1997

When I first set foot on the holy land that is known as Holy Trinity Monastery Jordanville, I had no idea I had encountered the miraculous living legacy of Saint Job of Pochaev. As I said earlier, I was tired from caregiving, and I was seeking the spiritual ethos of a great Monastery for refreshment. I must say, I got that and so much more. Who knew that the holy history of The Pochaev Icon came along with such a venerable

CHAPTER FIVE

Saint? And to think that this amazing Saint is available to befriend each of us, today!

During Saint Job's lifetime his exemplary piety moved many hearts to contribute generously. He did not have to twist anyone's arm to donate to his monastery. It was his holy life that naturally inspired people to do so. After the faithful got to know him, they were inspired. Their hearts were filled with the grace of God, so they did a lot to help. They contributed to the ornamentation of the church and helped the monastic brotherhood in any way necessary. People felt divine illumination pouring out of Saint Job. This reminds me of the blessedness I felt emanating from The Pochaev Icon when I first saw it. You don't need to read anything to sense this. You just know it in your heart. You simply feel this boundless sea of love. Deep down your soul knows you have encountered the gates of the Heavenly Kingdom.

One of the many wonderful achievements Saint Job did in his long life was the construction of a new stone church. This new stone church would replace the old wooden Church of the Dormition of the Mother of God. Saint Job could see that the wooden church was becoming inadequate in size to receive the many pilgrims coming to venerate The Pochaev Icon of the Mother of God. The number of pilgrims visiting The Pochaev Icon was growing day by day as its holy reputation spread throughout the region. The Saint worked together with the God-loving Domashevsky family to erect this new stone church on Mount Pochaev. It was

CHAPTER FIVE

dedicated to the All-Holy Trinity and this pious family paid for its construction.

The church was built a little higher than the original church of the Dormition, so that the rock ledge with the Theotokos' footprint was incorporated into the church itself. It is said that this idea was instigated by Saint Job himself. I love how the Saints help believers. Even in his new church design, Saint Job was working to make the Heavenly Kingdom accessible to us. He incorporated the footprint of the Mother of God in the new church so new generations of believers like you and me could encounter it even today.

In 1649, the church was completed. At the request of the Domashevsky donor family two side chapels were added. One was dedicated to the Annunciation of the Mother of God and the other to the Holy Great Martyr Theodore. In the very same year the church was consecrated, probably by Saint Job himself. He also moved the miracle-working Pochaev Icon of the Mother of God. It was transferred to the new church from the Church of the Dormition. Following Ancient Orthodox custom, it was placed on the iconostasis, above the royal doors of the main altar. A clever device was created allowing the icon to be lowered from its height, for greater accessibility when the faithful wished to venerate it. This amazing device is still in use in the catholicon of the Pochaev Lavra. Even with the icon up so high above the royal doors, at times the faithful are blessed with the chance to venerate the original Pochaev Icon up close and personal. When I first learned of this practice, it made me smile.

CHAPTER FIVE

This device mirrors what the Saints do for us. They come down, so to speak, from Heaven to be with us and pray for us when we call upon them.

The reliquary in the cave housing the relics of Saint Job of Pochaev, Defender of the Faith and The Pillar of Pochaev.

I just offered my mother's six-month memorial at Saint Petka Serbian Orthodox Church. My hope and prayer is that she, too, is up in Heaven with my father and grandparents. I am glad she is not suffering anymore. However, I still miss my Mama down here on earth. There is nothing like a mother's love. I often go into her empty apartment by myself and say aloud, *hi Mama, how are you*? I tell her I love her, and I also tell her to say hi to Daddy. And right before I leave, I also routinely stop in front of a large oil painting I made, years ago, of Russian Tsar-Martyr Nicholas II (1868-1918). It is not an icon, but instead a large life-size oil portrait of him. I also have an icon of him in my dining room. Because this man was a Tsar and now also a Great Martyr,

CHAPTER FIVE

sometimes, I say to myself, *talk to him*, Ariane. Maybe he has more pull with God. So, I ask the Tsar-Martyr for help.

I know this sounds funny perhaps, but this is how I think. I converse with our Saints. Sometimes I whisper a quick prayer or share a concern or worry with them. I say this even in front of a portrait or photo of them I have in my home. When I have more time, I pray in front of my icon wall and light my icon lamps. Sometimes, I ask the Tsar-Martyr to help my kids find Godly and wonderful future spouses. The other request I have made lately is to ask the Lord to help me write this book so that more people are strengthened in their belief in God through The Pochaev Icon and its miraculous history. Particularly while writing this chapter, I have thought about how much these two holy men — Saints Job and Tsar-Martyr Nicholas — have much in common.

Like Saint Job of Pochaev, Tsar-Martyr Nicholas was also connected to the Old Testament Job the Long-Suffering. The Tsar was born on the day in which the Holy Orthodox Church celebrates the memory of this Old Testament Saint. Saint Job of Pochaev received monastic tonsure with the name Job, after the very same Old Testament Saint. Both of these pious Saints were Orthodox leaders who feared God. One was the leader of a Monastery and the other the leader of an Empire. Though different kinds of leaders, they were both leaders of the Orthodox faith during very dark days. Both had the task to preserve the faith and help it grow. As such, they led their lives with the conscious

CHAPTER FIVE

awareness that they would have to answer to God one day for every deed. They also knew God had a reason for everything — even their suffering. Each accepted God's will like a lamb. The truth is, dying is easy. Living for Christ and a willingness to confess and preserve the Orthodox faith, come what may, is difficult. Thank God for giving us these two spiritual role models to show us the way. We need them now.

Recently I came across a written testimony that connects these Saints to The Pochaev Icon. Just a few weeks ago, before retiring for the evening, I decided to read some of the original 1913 diary of Tsar-Martyr Nicholas' eldest daughter, Grand Duchess-Martyr Olga Nikolaevna. I randomly came across her diary entry for February 17, 1913. And much to my surprise, Grand Duchess-Martyr Olga wrote that she had attended Liturgy with her family that day, and then further noted that The Pochaev Icon of the Mother of God had arrived in the afternoon and a short prayer service was held. My eyes stopped, glued to the page! Even though their holy lives were centuries apart, their lives crossed at one holy point preserved by God in time and space for future generations to see, thanks to Tsar-Martyr Nicholas' oldest daughter. Saint Job and Tsar- Martyr Nicholas II had both prayed before the same holy piece of matter. They had both stood in the presence of the same icon: The Pochaev Icon of the Mother of God.

Through time and space, God speaks to us in the form of these holy icons. Their earthly form is the Heavenly embodiment of the body of Christ. It's

CHAPTER FIVE

mind-boggling to imagine exactly who has gathered before these icons throughout the centuries. If we actually saw the list of holy people, we would be in awe. We would be speechless seeing the multitudes of righteous believers who have gotten down on their knees before these icons to venerate them and ask for the mercy of Our Almighty God. Seeing this scene continue throughout time, even into the future, would be transformational. Thoughts like these make me want to get down on my knees and weep for my sins. Sometimes our Holy Orthodox Faith is so big and so beautiful that our human minds cannot perceive the grandeur of such holiness.

While writing this book, I had the desire to put our Pochaev Icon of the Mother of God in a kiot (icon cabinet) to preserve it and keep it safe. A few months ago, I ordered one from a monastery in Minsk, Belarus. My order recently arrived. I opened the package, cleaned the glass door of the kiot, and then placed our icon inside the cabinet. After this, I secured it on my dining room icon wall. It looked so beautiful, bright, and clean compared to my other icons. One thing led to another, like the domino effect, and I started gently cleaning all the other icons on my icon wall. The very last one I prepared to clean was my icon of Tsar-Martyr Nicholas II (by the hand of iconographer, Janet Jaime). I was about to wipe it with a soft cloth but then I noticed something shiny under the Tsar-Martyrs's left eye. I swiped this away and suddenly realized it looked and felt like oil. So, I looked closely at his face, and saw that a single tear had streamed down his cheek emanating from his left eye.

CHAPTER FIVE

*The author's icon corner in her dining room:
The Pochaev Icon is in the kiot on the top far right;
Tsar-Martyr Nicholas II's icon is on the far left.*

I had never seen anything like this on any of my home icons. Suddenly I was bewildered, so I stopped and crossed myself. When I realized it was a tear, I immediately felt God's grace. At the same time, I have no idea what it meant. I asked my husband when he came home from work if he saw it and he did. Then a few days later, I asked my friend Elisa to come to my house to look at it. Maybe I was mistaken. Did I really see it? After Elisa saw it, she agreed there was a visible tear from his left eye. She encouraged me to contact Jordanville to see if there was anything I should do. I got in touch with the Director of Development for the Seminary, Father Deacon Michael Pavuk, who in turn asked Bishop Luke. His Grace responded by advising me to continue to just observe the icon. I love this response because it reminded me to keep

CHAPTER FIVE

The author and her friend and fellow pilgrim, Elisa Jackson, at Jordanville.

CHAPTER FIVE

looking with my spiritual eyes, but not to make any big deal or expect anything. Just observe holiness. In other words, from time to time don't forget to look for it.

I may never see the icon streaming myrrh (if it was) ever again. Or maybe I might. It really doesn't matter; what matters to me is I can still look at the icon up close and see the dried tear of the Tsar-Martyr. I don't even know what this tear means, but I do know that I feel encouraged and uplifted. My heart tells me, *God is with us!* The tear reminds me that holiness exists in every believer's home. We often forget that God uses matter in the work of our salvation. Sometimes God's grace reveals itself through physical realities such as holy icons, holy relics, or holy water. The only thing is, we must remember that without repentance and other Christian virtues, God's grace does not save. An icon becomes a useless talisman to unbelievers, or even Christians in name only, without any virtue.

It's interesting to note that this tear appeared while I was writing about Saint Job of Pochaev, an ardent defender of the Orthodox Faith. Just a few years ago, I wrote another book called *Debt of Love*, about Tsar-Martyr Nicholas II of Russia. I did this to pay back a debt of love to God for the Tsar-Martyr's Holy life. Tsar-Martyr Nicholas was chosen by God as His anointed to be the preserver of an Orthodox realm. Both of these Saints had the royal ministry of remaining steadfast and preserving Orthodoxy. Each helped the faith grow by their good deeds. I believe they continue to do so from Heaven. Maybe they look down at us and

CHAPTER FIVE

are sad that much of the world has forgotten God. I don't know what our Saints think. All I know is how seeing the tear made me feel. It felt like my Heavenly Friends, the Saints, were literally right next to me — keeping me close to Christ.

Before my friend Elisa left that day, she reminded me of something important. She said she felt that in time I would discover more meaningful revelations about my Tsar-Martyr icon and its tear. She was right. A miracle is not just what we see once. It's a spiritual gift that keeps on giving.

One day, I happened to check the Church calendar commemorations on either side of the day I first noticed the tear. I quickly discovered a feast day that every believer should commemorate, hold dear, and never forget. The Russian Orthodox Church celebrates the feast of the Holy New Martyrs and Confessors of Russia on the Sunday nearest January 25th (O.S.)/February 7th (N.S.) — the date Metropolitan Vladmir of Kiev's martyrdom (the first Hieromartyr of the Bolshevik Yoke). The 27th was when I touched the icon and felt it was still fluid but also a bit sticky. It felt as if it had streamed a few days earlier. Many describe January 25th as the feast day that commemorates Russia's second baptism. This feast reminds all believers to always remember and be inspired by the countless faithful who were baptized by the spilling of their blood.

Tsar-Martyr Nicholas II of Russia, his Tsaritsa-Martyr, four Grand Duchess Martyrs and Tsarevich-Martyr (heir apparent to the throne of the Russian Empire) were some of the very first who suffered persecution and death. But there were

CHAPTER FIVE

*On January 27, 2023, while writing this chapter,
the author discovered that a single tear had fallen from the
left eye of her Tsar-Martyr Nicholas II icon.
The icon is by the hand of iconographer Janet Jaime.*

many more to follow: metropolitans, monastics, archpriests, presidents of parishes, laity — everyone from royalty to peasants became martyrs. Millions upon millions of lives, known and unknown were lost under the demonic Marxist-Communist regime (1917-1991). These martyrs lived through an all-out war against God. They held firm to their Orthodox

CHAPTER FIVE

Faith, confessed Christ and did not give in. They remained steadfast — just like Saint Job of Pochaev. We need to learn from these heroes who stood strong against anti-Christian ideologies. We must ask them to help us in our present struggles. After all, why wouldn't we? They are now *victorious* — with and in Christ.

The Orthodox Church has many miracle-working icons. These icons are grace-filled lights that burn bright for each sincere pilgrim. Each window to Heaven stays open for believers and leaves its transformative breeze behind. Witnesses attest to their personal transformation. We must remember though, the grace of God most often happens in places where there is continuous prayer, such as in Churches: during the Divine Services, in the Mysteries (Sacraments) of the Church as well as before holy relics and holy icons. Throughout history The Pochaev Icon of the Mother of God and some of its copies have proven time and again to be an undeniable well-spring of miracles. It is important to remember that the miracles are not an end in themselves. *The greatest miracle is that we ourselves become transfigured in Christ.*

When I visited Jordanville and saw The Pochaev Icon of the Mother of God, I immediately knew this was a very special icon. I may not have seen any myrrh streaming, but I was drawn immediately to its holiness. Somehow, I knew it streams miracles. What an incredible treasure God has allowed us to encounter. I often reflect upon how people in Russia stand in line for countless hours to venerate miracle-working icons of the Mother of God. These

CHAPTER FIVE

believers know exactly who they are waiting in line for. They stand patiently for the Greatest Intercessor of all before the throne of God. How easy it is for many of us to hop in a car or plane and travel to New York to come venerate such an icon. And to think we don't even have to wait in line!

Life can be tough. Why do we so easily give up on hope when tribulations come into our lives? I often ask myself this question. The Pochaev Icon of the Mother of God has shown me that there is no such thing as a hopeless situation with God. And the venerable and Righteous Saint Job of Pochaev teaches all of us that we must get to know our Holy Orthodox Faith. Because when we truly know it, we understand our only hope is God. We must remember that He listens to His Mother. Then we will eagerly hop in a car or plane or wait in long lines to have an opportunity to venerate a holy image such as the miracle-working Pochaev Icon of the Mother of God. We will know we are nothing and nobody without God, and we will do anything and everything to seek Him.

When we know our faith like Saint Job, we will be filled with the desire to come venerate an icon like The Pochaev Icon of the Mother of God because we know the Theotokos is the joy and consolation of Christians. The Theotokos teaches us not to despair in sorrow but instead to trust the righteous judgement of God. She is the confirmation of the Orthodox Faith that Saint Job of Pochaev worked so hard to defend. Her miracle-working icons transfigure us. Through them, we are filled with rich spiritual treasures.

CHAPTER FIVE

In the next Chapter we will discuss some of the miracles of The Pochaev Icon of the Mother of God.

Jordanville's icon depicting Saint Job of Pochaev as a missionary, with his printing press and books in the background.

CHAPTER FIVE

*The majestic golden domes and crosses on
Holy Trinity Cathedral, Jordanville.
The Orthodox crosses shine bright in the New York horizon.
They inspire pilgrims that come to visit from around the world,
to place their hope and trust in
Our Lord and Savior Jesus Christ.*

CHAPTER SIX

REJOICE, O PRAISE OF POCHAEV, THE HOPE AND CONSOLATION OF THE WORLD.

OUR CROSS AND OUR MIRACLE: THE POCHAEV ICON OF THE MOTHER OF GOD

CHAPTER SIX

OUR CROSS AND OUR MIRACLE: THE POCHAEV ICON OF MOTHER OF GOD

As I begin writing this chapter, we have entered the midpoint of Great Lent. It arrived today with the Sunday of The Holy Cross. It is my first Lent without my mother. As time marches on, memories of the cross my mother and I shared together float back to me. The more I reflect, the more I see that cross was custom-made for Mama and me. Both of us faced that eleven-year journey together. We grew spiritually and suffered in our own unique ways. Like any cross, we could not run from it. We could not exchange it for another. God allowed this one just for us.

A cross means nothing without Christ. He transfigured this bit of matter and gave it back to us in its glory. When I gaze upon an Orthodox

CHAPTER SIX

*Matthias Grunewald's Western art depiction (left)
portrays Christ on the Cross writhing in pain.
The Russian Orthodox Icon of Christ on the Cross (right)
shows Christ standing almost serenely on the Cross.*

depiction of the Crucifixion, I feel uplifted. It radiates hope and peace. Many times in Western Crucifixion depictions you see the opposite. Christ is depicted as a contorted corpse nailed to the cross. You see agony and even blood. You look at these depictions and feel despair. Even in modern movies like Mel Gibson's *Passion of Christ* you see the same thing...terrible suffering. Viewers turn away in pain. You don't see the King of Glory or the Hope of the Resurrection.

When you look at Christ on the Cross in an Orthodox Church, you see Christ standing almost serenely on the Cross, instead of hanging on it. We are not confronted with a vision of pain. Instead, we rejoice at the vision of the Cross. Why? Because we know the Resurrection is coming. The Cross has become something new for us. A compass

CHAPTER SIX

that points us to the Kingdom of Heaven. We cannot think of the Cross without remembering the Resurrection; Christ's death has no meaning without His Resurrection.

Christ accepted His Cross willingly for us. He accepted ridicule, hatred, betrayal, and ultimately death so we could all receive life. He carried upon himself the heavy sins of humanity. Saint Theophan the Recluse once said, "The chief end of our life is to live in communion with God. To this end the Son of God became incarnate, to return us to this divine communion, which was lost by the fall into sin. Through Jesus Christ, the Son of God, we enter into communion with the Father and thus attain our purpose."

The only way to survive any of our crosses in life is with our Lord and Savior Jesus Christ, The King of Glory. During our tough times, it's easy to forget He is right there with us. A few months before Mama's illness began, she had an unforgettable dream. The next morning, she told me to come to her home immediately. She indicated that she had to share this dream with me right away and that it even scared her a bit. In the first part of the dream, she saw her long departed Serbian Aunt Rada (whose Father was a Serbian Orthodox priest). Aunt Rada implored her to quickly wake up, sit up, and face the blindingly bright light in the corner of her bedroom. Mama explained to me she loved the light when she saw it but also feared it at the same time. She said the light began to speak to her. It said, Danica, why do you know *of* me and but don't *know* me?

CHAPTER SIX

Radmila Dragović, Ariane's mother's favorite aunt, strolling with Danica in Beograd/Belgrade. Rada is the aunt who came to Danica in a dream before her illness.

CHAPTER SIX

As she continued to describe her dream I sat in front of her speechless. I knew this was something big. Not only was I at a loss for words, but I immediately felt that the bright light must be Our Lord and Savior Jesus Christ. My strong-willed mother had stubbornly held on to some almost silly grudges in life. One of them was her neighbor whose front door you saw the minute you left Mama's home. She was not on speaking terms with her neighbor because the neighbor had complained about her dog barking a time or two. Mama told me that if I ever spoke to her neighbor, she would be very angry with me. She even went so far as to say that if I talked to this neighbor, she would disown me (I must say here that sometimes Balkan women can be a bit dramatic.). This created a lot of awkwardness when I pulled my car onto my mother's driveway to visit. How could I not wave and be friendly to her neighbors? Mama said the bright light in her dream spoke to her in a reprimanding tone and said that when she leaves her home she must always be cheerful and kind to everyone she sees — without exception. There was more to her dream, but it struck me how the Lord loved her so much as to come to correct her. As I reflect upon our experience together, it's clear that God was with us in the smallest of details from the very start of our cross. On top of that, both of us got to know Him and love Him and submit to His will throughout the many years of our struggle together.

I have no doubt that my mother would agree with me now when I say we are both so grateful for

CHAPTER SIX

the cross we endured together. God was merciful to give us a special time together to get to know Him better. The crosses we bear in our lives really do help restore our faith in God. They transfigure us. When I look back on all the challenges and dramas in taking care of Mama, I no longer feel stress, anger, or fear. Now all I feel is love and peace. This cross of mine taught me to consistently strive to give myself over to the will of God so that He may guide me as He sees fit. And whatever affliction comes my way in the future, I will strive to have confidence in God alone and remember I am never alone in suffering, sickness, or sorrow.

After all, no one on this earth can avoid afflictions. If we call upon Him in our time of trouble, God in His great mercy will hear us. I have come to learn that everything turns out well when I include God in my plans. He sees and knows all things in our lives. We will never lose heart if we trust in the Lord. He loves us. He created us. He is the Master of our lives. He steers us. I finally understand that although I have free will, I am not the master of my life — not even in the littlest things. God is.

About eight years into my caregiving journey, I stopped wondering how much longer Mama and I were to endure this tribulation together. I had imagined it for so long. How would it happen and when. Over and over, I tried to picture how I would react when she died. Would I be ready? Her end had been near so many times. After numerous health challenges, she remained with us. Even the hospice nurse said she had never had a bed-ridden patient live as long as my mother. In fact, I had her

CHAPTER SIX

handmade coffin stored in my garage over a decade before her actual repose. One day I finally began to let go of my fears and surrendered to God's will. It was not for me to know the hour or time of Mama's death.

My job was to trust and endure with Christ leading us. I could not rearrange God's will. As much as I loved to control and organize things neatly in life, I realized I was not in charge. God gave me no sign how much longer we had to endure this cross. In the past, when I cried out to God, I sort-of demanded to know why this was so long for both of us. When, I stopped questioning, my heart calmed down. I began to trust God's plan and remember every part of this journey was needed for our salvation.

When I look back now, I say to myself, how could I have questioned God and His love for us? Nothing is accidental by His hand. Around this time of letting go I began to reflect upon His miracles. Reading about each one gave me a lot of peace. Our Lord and Savior Jesus Christ's miracles are a chain of golden gifts for all of us suffering our crosses. They should be enough to help us through anything. The miracles of the Lord teach us. They show us His unlimited power. A power that is enough to make our hearts rest easy.

God has given us all we need to know Him. And when we get to know Him, we can get through anything. He is our God of abundant love and mercy. He pours out His grace upon all. Every year when Pascha rolls around, I find myself weeping with joy when I hear the Homily of Saint John

CHAPTER SIX

Chrysostom. In part of it he says, **"The table is full-laden; feast ye all sumptuously. The calf is fatted; let no one go hungry away. Enjoy ye all the feast of faith: Receive ye all the riches of loving-kindness. Let no one bewail his poverty, for the universal Kingdom has been revealed!"**

Those riches of the universal Kingdom Saint John speaks of were first revealed to us at Christ's inaugural miracle at the wedding in Cana of Galilee. It was the Mother of God who taught us at that first miracle. She taught us exactly *Who* is the Way, the Truth, and the Life, by saying, *"Do whatever He says."* Her four simple words tell us all we need to know. The reality though is that we humans take baby steps. We forget to do whatever our Lord and Savior says. We forget to call upon Him. We question Him. For us its one step forward and two steps back. In His great mercy, God gives us the fullness of the Orthodox Church to survive our difficulties and confusion. I love that the Orthodox Church glorifies the Mother of God daily. This continual remembrance of Her is a great comfort for anyone and everyone. It forever reminds us that in His great mercy God gave us a Heavenly Mother to turn to. She sees our every tear and lifts us up through our tribulations.

In his ceaseless devotion to the Mother of God throughout the entirety of his life, Saint Job of Pochaev illustrates the great spiritual importance of the Theotokos. Saint Job always called upon the Most Holy Mother of God when help was needed because he knew his pleas would be heard. Even after his death, his successors like Abbot

CHAPTER SIX

Joseph Dobromirsky continued to urge brethren and laypeople to turn to the Theotokos and pray fervently for help. These holy men knew how spiritually powerful it is to diligently seek divine intervention from the Mother of God. Even in desperate times such as war, they knew She could step in and help stop any calamity. After all, She is called our Champion Leader and Protectress for a reason. She even tells us how spiritually important She is for all humanity: **"For He hath regarded the low estate of his handmaiden: for behold, from henceforth all generations shall call me blessed." (Luke 1:48, KJV)**

From one generation to the next, we see that there are certain places on earth that are favored by the Mother of God herself. The Pochaev Lavra in Ukraine has historically proved to be one of Her places. They say there is no Christian without a cross. Even though the Theotokos favors Pochaev as Her divine abode, it hasn't always been easy for those living there. This area has experienced a generous share of tribulations. As we previously touched upon, in the year of 1721, the formerly Orthodox population of Pochaev was forced into the Unia or Eastern-Rite Catholicism. Even in this difficult time for the Lavra, the Monastery chronicle notes 539 miracles attributed to this glorified Orthodox icon.

During the second half of the century, a Uniate nobleman, Count Nicholas Pototski, became an unexpected Monastery benefactor through a Pochaev Icon miracle he experienced. One day he angrily accused his coachman of overturning

CHAPTER SIX

his carriage with reckless horses. Count Nicholas reached for his gun and intended to shoot his coachman. The coachman suddenly turned towards Pochaev Hill, threw his hands upwards and cried out: "Mother of God, manifest in the Pochaev Icon and save me!"

Pototski tried to shoot the pistol but it kept misfiring. He was completely bewildered. This weapon had never failed him before. The coachman stood before him alive. How could this be? Pototski was dumbfounded. After that miracle, he went to venerate The Pochaev Icon of the Mother of God. Shortly thereafter he decided to devote his life to building up the Monastery. He took his wealth and built the Dormition Cathedral and other buildings for the brethren. The Mother of God heard the coachman's prayers.

After this, more good news came. Pochaev returned to the bosom of Orthodoxy in 1832. This was precipitated by the miraculous healing of a blind woman named Anna Akimchukova. She had come on pilgrimage to the holy Pochaev Icon of the Mother of God with her seventy-year-old grandmother who lived a few hours away from Pochaev. In memory of her miraculous healing from blindness, the Volynia archbishop and Lavra Archimandrite Innokenty (1832-1840) instituted Saturday weekly services of the cathedral Akathist before the Wonderworking Pochaev Icon. During the time of the Archbishop of Volynia, Archimandrite Agathangel's rule over the Lavra, a separate chapel was constructed in the gallery of the Holy Trinity Church, in memory of the

CHAPTER SIX

victory over the Tatars. It was consecrated on July 23, 1875.

When you begin to pray the Akathist to the Most Holy Theotokos in honor of Her Wonderworking Icon of Pochaev (one is included at the end of this book) a holy transformation takes place in your heart. If you stick to it, you will really get to know the Mother of God. You will see how She is working to protect us from evil and lead us to Her Son. There is something that happens when you stay focused on an Akathist prayer. Without it you really miss the spiritual connection you have with Her. I know if I stop for any reason or forget to do it for some time — suddenly I feel different. Even if someone only does the prayer at the end of the Akathist, that person will feel uplifted and comforted. You also get to know the history of the Mother of God as it is manifested through Her miracle-working Pochaev Icon. For example, when you read Kondak 10 (a Kondak, or Kondakion is a form of hymn performed in the Orthodox Church), you hear about the aforementioned story of blind Anna.

Kondak 10

Seeking the salvation of a simple woman blinded by false teachings, O most Pure Theotokos, thou didst move her young granddaughter, blind in her eyes from birth but illumined with the Light of Orthodoxy, to implore her to bring her to venerate this, thy holy Image on the Mountain of Pochaev. And when they came

CHAPTER SIX

> before thee, O Lady, the blind girl was healed and her grandmother was taught to proclaim the Orthodox Faith and she sang to God: Alleluia!

When you absorb the story, time and again you remember that not only was a blind person healed, but that the Mother of God is alive in the Heavenly Kingdom. We all need to feel the love of our Heavenly Mother. In addition, when we pray the Akathist, we feel her love and compassion for us. We remember that She is watching us from the heights of Heaven and working to guide us onto the path of righteousness. Reading the Akathist simply benefits our souls. It is a little miracle we can partake in every day by spending time with the Theotokos.

And the truth is why wouldn't we? We have so many empty moments every day that we fill with nothingness. We can always find a little time to spend with the Theotokos. Perhaps if you keep this little book with you throughout the day, you will find those moments. It can be as simple as a moment praying the Akathist in the car waiting for your child to come out of class, on your morning walk or even on the tail end of a lunch break before returning to work. Why not commune and get to know this steadfast advocate for us before Christ? We can ask the Theotokos for big things and little things. The history of The Pochaev Icon of the Mother of God has shown us miracles and wonders do stream to people who come before the icon. The

CHAPTER SIX

icon is on the front cover of this book. If we look at the front cover of this book and cross ourselves before Her Pochaev Icon, we will start our prayer by remembering exactly who we are addressing. After that, we can proceed to pray the Akathist with love and humility. Whenever we do this prayer, we are opening the door to Paradise. No matter where we are praying, *She is with us*.

She graciously accepts our intercessory prayers and takes them to the throne of God. The question is then, why don't we pray more often? I ask myself this when I forget to do so for long stretches of time. Then I feel despondency creeping in. We have this tremendous spiritual blessing God gives us in the Theotokos. We have Her to help us in our lives and also the life of the world. As I write, there is a war raging between two brother nations, Russia and Ukraine. They share a holy and beautiful spiritual history. Many might not know that they descended from one Orthodox Christian root, Kievan Rus'. How utterly tragic for brothers to fight! The news constantly comments on the horrors and fuels the fires of hatred. Some say this battle could escalate into World War III. We continue to shake our heads in sadness at media reports. We talk and talk about who is to blame. These conversations produce nothing. And all we know is the blood shed continues.

We need to remind ourselves that this conflict really is a spiritual battle. Often, we forget that the evil one exists and satan loves nothing more than destruction, bloodshed, and death. People in this day and age forget that satan's demons do still inhabit

CHAPTER SIX

people. He loves to take down God-fearing nations and pious families. They are his prime targets.

You know the evil one hates the beautiful words of Saint John Chrysostom, "The love of a husband and wife is the force that welds society together." Look at what satan did by using Lenin and his cronies to brutally murder the last meek and humble Imperial family of the Romanov Dynasty. Tsar-Martyr Nicholas II and his beloved wife Tsaritsa-Martyr Alexandra had a beautiful marriage and loving family life. The family was God-fearing and led their nation by their harmonious example of holy family life. They were literally slaughtered by people who hate God. This Orthodox family was, and still is, a role model for believers. They show us how to live a loving, pure, and harmonious Christian family life. But satan hates harmony and love. His targets are Godly families and nations. Division and hatred is the ultimate tactic and weapon of the evil one who desires nothing more than seeing two brother nations war and hate each other. The truth is satan delights when hatred and dissention exist. I pray that none of us give in to the evil one anymore. When we criticize and complain about any war, we get nowhere. Why fan the fire of division?

The truth is God allows worldwide crosses such as wars, in order for us to return to Him. As we look around the world, we see once holy and exemplary nations have slipped away from God. As a result, they become prime targets for satan. Our only hope now is divine help. Instead of talking, I, myself need to begin to pray for this war to end. Maybe you readers can also join me and pray. Instead of talking

CHAPTER SIX

about it, let's pray for an end. We don't need to wait for world leaders or politicians. We are the ones who can restore love and harmony in the world by asking the Pochaev Mother of God for help. We have already learned what she has successfully achieved in the past in this tumultuous area of the world. Each of us must strive to possess the confidence of Saint Job of Pochaev that She will hear our petitions. Our hope and prayer is that She intercedes for these nations on our behalf.

Can you imagine all of us becoming a groundswell of people coming together and praying for these two brother nations? A fellowship of believers focused on praying to The Pochaev Mother of God, just like Saint Job of Pochaev did so long ago. Many say that history repeats itself. So why not ask the Mother of God Pochaev to intervene? If we ask the Mother of God in faith and love to soften hearts, this war can end. Let us strive for the faith of Saint Job, so we can say, "Lord, I believe you can end this war; help my unbelief!"

On a personal level, writing Chapter Six has been eye-opening for me. I did not initially see the connection between current and past events in Ukraine concerning this icon. And now it seems so obvious. I am writing a book about this miraculous icon and until now I had not even thought to pray to the Mother of God about stopping this war. After all, the Pochaev Mother of God Icon resides in the Pochaev Lavra, which is in Ukraine. This is her chosen area of the world. Instead of sharing my opinions to others on any world tribulations, from this time forward I will pray to the Pochaev

Theotokos not only for my life, but also for the life of the world.

Perhaps those of you who read this book might take a moment and come together in fellowship with a family member or friend to pray. This way we can ask for Her divine intervention to end this bloodshed! The revelation I experienced this past Sunday in church when I heard a Kontakion inspired me to begin to pray to the Theotokos to end this war. After all, The Pochaev Icon of the Mother of God is the protector of Ukraine.

> **Kontakion of the Sundays of Great Lent Plagal of the Fourth Tone**
>
> To Thee, our Captain, Queen of war and battle trophies won, thy people rescued by thine aid from peril, dedicate as our offering of thanksgiving, O Theotokos, as thou hast might which none by war can overcome, from all forms of danger hast though delivered me, that I may cry unto thee: Hail, O Virgin, unwedded bride.

I pray that each of you readers might join me in praying to end the war now raging between two brother nations, Russia and Ukraine. Let's join together in praying the Akathist to the Mother of God at the end of this book, to cast the forces of the evil one out of this area.

Many times, we only focus on praying for ourselves and our families. We ask the Mother of God in prayer to go to battle for those near and dear

CHAPTER SIX

to us that are in our immediate proximity. I often forget about the rest of the world. I am inspired when people remember to pray for others beyond their immediate circle, or when someone gives someone else a holy gift that leads other people to pray for even more people. Like dominos, these grace-filled prayers keep on moving and touching others. This is the best kind of gift. I recently heard of someone who did just that. It was John Keller, a Holy Trinity Seminary graduate and Reader from Jordanville. In January 2023, he decided to give a special Christmas gift to his Assistant Parish priest back home in Saint Andrew Stratelates Cathedral, in Saint Petersburg, Florida. John had heard this priest's wife had recently been suffering from the discomfort of an illness.

John knew firsthand that the miracle-working copy of The Pochaev Icon at Jordanville is known for miraculous healings, especially for women's health issues. He decided to send his assistant parish priest a small bottle of blessed holy oil from the ever-burning lampada (icon lamp) in front of the Jordanville copy of The Pochaev Icon of the Mother of God. Holy oils like The Pochaev Icon holy oil are another blessing for us from God. One way to think of them is as a spiritual medicine. They are special medicines God gives us for psychological, physical, and spiritual healing. Get one of these bottles for yourself and anoint yourself and your loved ones frequently and say a brief prayer to the Pochaev Mother of God and ask for Her intercessory prayers. This way divine grace from our Lord can touch you and your family. I encourage every reader to order

CHAPTER SIX

this Pochaev Icon Holy oil from the Monastery bookstore at **https://bookstore.jordanville.org**.

In addition to sending the holy oil, John also included an icon of the Pochaev Mother of God in the gift package, so the Matushka (a priest's wife) could venerate the icon before or after being anointed with the holy oil. He did not expect to hear what happened next. After his gift was received, it was given to the grateful Matushka. But sometime in January of 2023 the priest was inspired to share The Pochaev Icon holy oil with a few of his parishioners in need of healing.

One such person was a middle-aged lady who was mentally disabled and had gotten ill quite suddenly. In fact, she was so ill she had stopped eating and had not eaten in two weeks. As a result, her family decided to put her on hospice care. Everyone thought her end had come. The priest was called in by the family for the departure of soul prayers. When he came, he prayed and decided to anoint her with The Pochaev Icon holy oil he had received from John. To everyone's surprise, the lady was very responsive to the holy oil anointing. Not only did her eyes open, but three days after his visit the family called to share good news. She had recovered and was completely back to normal.

Another miracle from John's gift of holy oil began to stream forth. It concerned a young boy. His mother was inconsolable because her son had been diagnosed with a tumor in his head that was inoperable. The very same priest went to visit and pray for this sick young boy. Once again, he decided

CHAPTER SIX

Reader John Keller holding a bottle of holy oil from the lampada (icon lamp) of the Jordanville Pochaev Icon of the Mother of God, while standing next to it. John sent a bottle of this holy oil to his home parish in Saint Petersburg Florida, where clergy prayerfully anointed two parishioners.

CHAPTER SIX

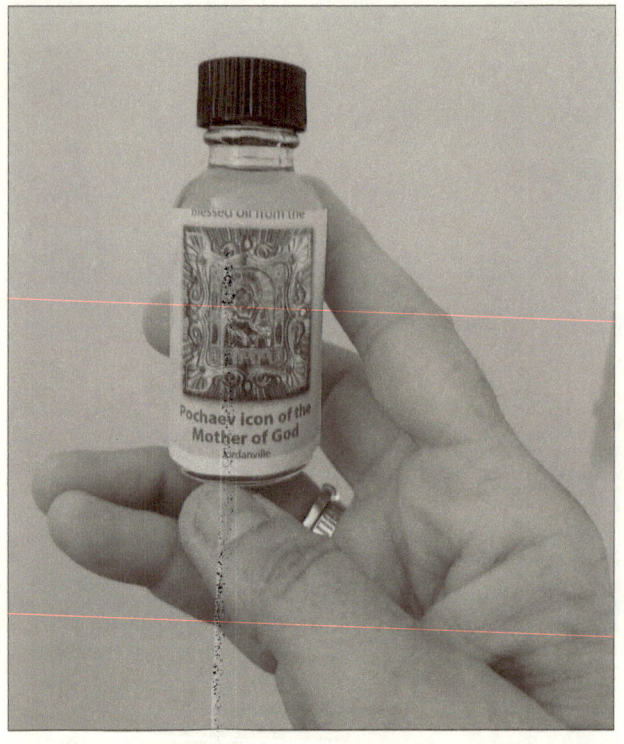

Readers can purchase bottles of holy oil from the Jordanville copy of The Pochaev Icon of the Mother of God lampada (icon lamp) from the Monastery bookstore at:
https://bookstore.jordanville.org.

CHAPTER SIX

to anoint him with The Pochaev Icon holy oil. Again, good news followed. His family was overjoyed when shortly after this anointing he went in for an MRI and they discovered the tumor had completely disappeared! Whether you call this a miracle or not, it is clear the Mother of God went to battle for this lady and young boy's health and asked Her Son our Lord and Savior Jesus Christ to heal them. Again, it begs the question, why wouldn't any of us ask for Her prayers?

While writing this Chapter, I recently bumped into a friend of mine from Church. She told me about her pregnant goddaughter who is a newlywed. The goddaughter was recently diagnosed with cancer. I don't know her, but I believe the Mother of God can help her if God allows it. As Christ taught us when he said **"where two or three are gathered together in my name, there am I in the midst of them," (Matthew 18:20, KJV)**, my friend and I will travel to visit this young woman and say the Akathist prayers to the Pochaev Mother of God. We will also bring her gifts of the holy oil and an icon of The Pochaev Mother of God from Jordanville. I am grateful to John Keller for the inspiration to do this. We will also encourage this young woman to visit Jordanville and venerate The Pochaev Icon and ask for healing. We as believers can all work together and set our hearts aflame with love and reverence for the Theotokos. If we have hope in the Queen of Heaven and earth, I truly believe anything is possible.

There are so many wonderful stories where we learn how wonderworking icons are miraculously

CHAPTER SIX

taken to where there is a need. The Mother of God is always our help and sometimes She comes right to us wherever we live. She knows where to go.

My friend Masha told me all about such a holy occurrence with The Pochaev Icon of the Mother of God. One of her dear longtime friends came to visit Jordanville one day and stayed with her family for the night. She had not seen her friend in almost 30 years. He told her all about a miracle his dad experienced after an encounter with the Jordanville Pochaev Icon of the Mother of God. He told Masha that sometime in the 1980s, his father was diagnosed with colon cancer and the prognosis was grim. At that time, The Pochaev Icon happened to be traveling in the greater northeast area of the United States visiting several churches. It was not scheduled to stop in the area where Masha's friend and father lived. Out of the blue, the two Jordanville monks that were traveling with the icon felt a sudden urge to stop and visit the parish church where this man belonged. This was in Nyack, New York. They both felt that the Mother of God wanted them to stop in this parish church. They contacted the priest and asked if there was anyone in the parish who needed a visit from The Pochaev Icon of the Mother of God. The priest immediately mentioned Masha's friend's father, so the monks, along with the parish priest, took The Pochaev Icon to the father. They served a special service for the sick before the icon. A few days later, the man was scheduled for major surgery to remove the cancer from his colon. They opened him up, only to discover his cancer was

CHAPTER SIX

The author and her church friend, Sue Parsons, took a bottle of Pochaev Icon holy oil and a Pochaev Icon blessed copy from Jordanville to a young woman. Together, they prayed the Akathist to the Most Holy Theotokos in honor of Her Wonderworking Icon of Pochaev for the healing of their friend. Now this young lady is cancer-free.

not as serious as they thought. The cancer had not spread as previous tests indicated it surely would. After this miracle, this man lived for many years cancer-free. In fact, he lived to a ripe old age and reposed in 2019.

We will never know the details of this man's prayer life. My heart tells me that this believer must have prayed fervently for the Mother of God to intercede for his healing. The result was that the Theotokos made it known to the two monks that she wanted her Pochaev Icon to make an extra stop at his house. If there's anything I have learned from this long journey with Mama, it is to stay

CHAPTER SIX

devoted in fervent prayer to our Lord Jesus Christ, and His Saints.

Every morning I take my little doggie named Hugo for a walk in the park. I make a point to stop halfway through the walk to take two small icons out of my backpack and prop them up so I can pray before them.

The author's dog Hugo.

I get out two blessed icon cards you can get from the Jordanville Monastery bookstore. (The Pochaev Icon of the Mother of God and Saint Job of Pochaev). Then I take out my Prayer to the Theotokos which I copied from the last pages of the Pochaev Akathist at the end of this book. I had the icon cards and the prayer laminated, so that if it rains I don't worry about the icon cards smudging. I say the Prayer to

CHAPTER SIX

the Most Holy Theotokos (pages 258, 259, and 260 in this book) and after that the Troparion to The Pochaev Icon of the Mother of God (page 260 and 261 in this book), followed by the Fourth tone to Saint Job of Pochaev. It goes like this:

> **Troparion, Fourth Tone**
> Having acquired the patience of thy longsuffering forefather, and having resembled the Baptist in abstinence, and having shared the divine zeal of both, thou wast vouchsafed to receive their names; and thou wast a fearless preacher of the true Faith. In this way thou didst bring a multitude of monastics to Christ; and thou didst strengthen all the people in Orthodoxy, O Job, our holy father, pray that our souls be saved.

I feel comforted whenever I pray to Saint Job of Pochaev. After all, Saint Job of Pochaev had such a great devotion to the Pochaev Theotokos. And we know She listened and responded to him. Even in times of war, She heard his persistent prayers. His lifetime was filled with never-ending spiritual struggles against the true faith. And now we are faced with the very same challenges worldwide. We need Saint Job's prayers right now. Just this week, I learned that the Kiev-Pechersk Lavra is under attack by the evil one. It is one of the largest Orthodox sanctuaries in the world — especially in its spiritual stature. This is why it has been the target of atheists

CHAPTER SIX

for a thousand years and counting. What better Saint to pray for this spiritual turmoil than Saint Job? After all, he lived through all of this during his own time. He comes to mind because he knows that the darkness which surrounds this venerable monastery and its faithful cannot and will not be stronger than the power of God! With the Mother of God Pochaev and Saint Job of Pochaev praying for us, we have powerful intercessors on our side. With their help, our windows to Heaven remain open in our lives. This Godless world cannot and will not overtake us believers. The only thing we must continue to do is pray, pray, pray.

Not long after this thought, I was back on my morning walk pondering these Saints and spiritual thoughts a bit more. As I crossed a small bridge with my doggie, I saw a beautiful sight approaching. Out of the blue I saw a husband and wife walking towards me with three gorgeous Siberian Huskies. The eyes of these dogs were so incredibly blue! One of these huskies in particular stood out. I could not help staring at it! His radiant eyes pulled me in! The lady said, I see you like him. I said yes, I do like him very much. I detected an accent as she spoke. Since I come from a Serbian family I can guess Serbian and Russian accents pretty quickly and determine the difference. Plus, it also helps that my mother spoke Russian. I quickly asked the lady if she was Russian. The lady affirmed she was, and I mentioned my parents were Serbian. Then she said you will understand the meaning of this dog's name. It is Chuda. Yes, I replied, the word means

CHAPTER SIX

miracle! I knew this word because it is the same word in Serbian, only spelled slightly different.

I will never forget the story she began to tell, which explained why she named him Chuda. She said Chuda was the last of the litter to be born. She was assisting in the delivery with a few other people. The Siberian pup came out looking stillborn. She said he looked absolutely lifeless. Everyone present at his delivery agreed that there was no hope for the last one. This was the consensus: it was a successful litter except for one. However, the lady standing before me decided there was hope, so she persisted in trying to help the pup. She was the only one who kept on massaging his chest non-stop. Five, ten, fifteen minutes passed. She kept on trying, but to no avail. He was limp. One person present even said he is dead. But this lady said, "no, no, no — no giving up! We must continue to try," and she did. Miraculously, after several more minutes he began moving ever so slightly and then, suddenly, came fully back to life. It was at that joyous moment she gave him the name miracle: Chuda!

My recent encounter with Chuda, the Siberian Husky and his persistent and loving human mother, who never gave up, touched me deeply. I immediately felt the true meaning of miracles in Chuda's story. We should not marvel about the specific phenomenon of the miracle itself. Instead, we need to regard every miracle simply as a spiritual opening. A way of entering in, to acquiring the steadfast hope and knowledge that our great Lord God and His Saints are always right there for us. This is especially true if we continually persist in

CHAPTER SIX

The author, Siberian Husky Chuda, and his mother.

our faith. Miracles in our lives are a great mystery of God. All we can do is accept them with grateful hearts. It is not for us to question God. Or to say who gets a miracle, or why, or why not. This is a very personal matter. Only God knows all the reasons why. Our jobs are to continue to be fervent in prayer, faith, hope, and love.

If there's anything I've learned from this long journey with Mama is to stay devoted and persistent in prayer like Saint Job of Pochaev. He never gave up even in life's darkest times. Hope in Christ makes you never give up. Saint Job of Pochaev absolutely knew when we turn to the Theotokos for help, that is when our real miracle

CHAPTER SIX

*Jordanville's icon of Saint Job of Pochaev holding
The Pochaev Icon of the Mother of God.
He remained devoted in prayer to the Theotokos his entire life —
no matter what tribulation came his way.*

THE POCHAEV ICON • 209

CHAPTER SIX

begins. She brings us back to Her Son, Our God. When we come face to face with the Queen of Heaven and earth, the door to Christ opens. She is the Ardent Intercessor who helps us fulfill our life purpose. She helps us return to and reunite with Her Son, Our Lord and Savior Jesus Christ. With Christ we can bear any cross! Amen!

Rejoice, O Profound comfort of all the faithful.

Rejoice, O Praise of Pochaev, the Hope and Consolation of the world.

Most Holy Mother of God save and protect all who read this book!

CHAPTER SIX

Ariane and her Mama
MEMORY ETERNAL!
DANICA VELIBOR DOBRIĆ TRIFUNOVIĆ
(January 31, 1932-June 28, 2022)

CHAPTER SEVEN

*REJOICE, O PRAISE OF POCHAEV,
THE HOPE AND CONSOLATION
OF THE WORLD.*

GOD'S MIRACULOUS GIFTS: JORDANVILLE AND ITS POCHAEV ICON OF THE MOTHER OF GOD

CHAPTER SEVEN

GOD'S MIRACULOUS GIFTS: JORDANVILLE AND ITS POCHAEV ICON OF THE MOTHER OF GOD

The timing of my arrival at the final chapter of this book is divine. Pascha is at our doorstep. Today is Palm Sunday. As I listened to the Divine Liturgy this morning, the last few words of the Kontakion of Palm Sunday touched me. They rested deeply in my heart: *Blessed art Thou, O Lord, Who didst come to call back Adam from the dead.* Wow. God came to call us back to Him. He loves each and every one of us, *all the way back to Adam*! In a split second my heart sensed how immeasurable God's love for all of us is.

Time marches on in this temporary world. Great Lent ends and Holy Week begins. As each year fades into the next, Great Lent beckons every believer to

CHAPTER SEVEN

strive to increase their love for God and lessen their love for worldly passions. I began to ponder my current spiritual state as Holy Week began. With Mama gone almost a year, I can clearly see how our cross bore great spiritual fruit in my life. I finally realized that God *was* always and is *always* there for me. He will *forever* be at my side. As long as I turn to Him, worry or despondency won't be my companions. Suddenly, the Epistle for Palm Sunday rang out and brought my mind back to the Liturgy: "Blessed is He Who comes in the Name of the Lord. Give thanks to the Lord, for He is good. His mercy endures forever."

As I took in each word, a church friend next to me, Linda Bell, suddenly leaned in and pointed to the church bulletin I was holding open. She directed me to the reading for Palm Sunday and whispered quickly, "Ariane, look at what's being read next; these words inspire me to no end!" Her prompting made me feel as if the Holy Spirit was saying *pay attention, Ariane, you need to hear this*! Thanks to her, I became attentive, and this is what I heard:

> **Brethren, rejoice in the Lord always; again, I will say, Rejoice. Let all men know your forbearance. The Lord is at hand. Have no anxiety about anything. But in everything by prayer and supplication with thanksgiving let your requests be made known to God. And the peace of God, which passes all understanding, will keep your hearts and your minds in Christ pure, whatever is lovely, whatever is gracious, if**

CHAPTER SEVEN

there is any excellence, if there is anything worthy of praise, think about these things. What you have learned and received and heard and seen in me, do; and the God of peace will be with you.
                       Philippians 4:4-9 (KJV)

I listened carefully and felt God's immeasurable love for us. I thought of all the miraculous gifts He gives us including our friends in Christ — the Saints. All the gifts He gives help restore our relationship with Him. Then out of the blue, my thoughts were drawn back to one of these miraculous gifts: The Pochaev Icon of the Mother of God. I saw myself back in time standing right before this beautiful icon. I remember feeling as if my heart would explode. Love and peace surrounded me. Earthly cares were gone. Even now, I am not motherless, because the Theotokos is my Heavenly Mother. And when I saw the jewelry left behind by struggling believers, I felt that these were my people. All of us were seeking help that only God could provide. Each of us needed Our Father's all-encompassing love. After all, we are loved at *all times* by God and His Saints. Especially during trying times in life, we forget that God is with us. When we let go and turn to Him, we are home.

The peace that passes all understanding is within everyone's reach, and all we need to do is repent: *Lord Jesus Christ, Son of God, have mercy upon me, a sinner.* Those twelve simple words help remind each of us that we can survive anything from now on, if we only realign ourselves to the Lord through

CHAPTER SEVEN

repentance. When I do this, I am reminded that *the Kingdom of God is at hand*. Sometimes in our everyday lives we forget how very close the Kingdom of God really is. But again, we should not worry, because the good news is that the Church is there to remind us.

God gives us everything we need in the Orthodox Church to remember that His Kingdom is at hand. Christ Himself tells us that the Kingdom of God is within us. It is in our *hearts*. This is where we unite ourselves in obedience to our Lord God. Seek first the Kingdom of Heaven and the peace of God will enter our hearts. The Kingdom of God leads us the right way to Righteous glory or *Pravoslav* (Slavonic).

The Kingdom of God is present at every Orthodox Divine Liturgy. The Lord gives us miraculous spiritual gifts in abundance within the Church that lead us to Him. We have our icons — like The Pochaev Icon of the Mother of God — so we can see and venerate the Kingdom of God. We have spiritual medicines in the tangible form of holy oil and holy water. We have our beautiful churches which are hospitals for our souls. We must also remember our Orthodox Monasteries. I like to call them the *big guns* because they are a huge *spiritual* threat to the evil one and his legions.

People often forget that we lay people can visit our Orthodox Monasteries. In fact, we need to visit holy places and donate to them to help them grow — *now more than ever*. Jordanville is a double threat to the evil one because Jordanville has a Monastery and a Seminary. Thank God for the continual Church services and spiritual education that take

CHAPTER SEVEN

place there. We would be in trouble if there were no more Orthodox monasteries and seminaries in the world. Truth be told, the numbers are dwindling because the world has turned its back on God.

On the bright side, we who love God strive to build His Kingdom. After all, He gives us so many gifts to draw us back to Him. The Pochaev Icon of the Mother of God is one of many we gratefully receive. Through it the Theotokos shines Her holy presence and prayers in our lives. It's only natural for us to feel the need to express our gratitude and give back. That is why I decided to write this book as a fundraiser for Holy Trinity Seminary. I have no doubt God sees us when we work together to help build His Kingdom. **www.hts.edu/support**

Sometimes I like to imagine that when we die, God will ignore our sins and say instead, is that someone who tried to help an Orthodox Monastery? Let's do this together. It is a holy honor to do so. We donate to help our local Churches but oftentimes forget about our Orthodox monasteries. You know the old saying, "out of sight, out of mind." Holy Trinity Monastery and Seminary may be out of sight, but it is important to remember that the monastics are praying for us day and night. They are silently battling evil on our behalf and on behalf of the world. There have been great holy men too numerous to count, who have passed through the doors at Jordanville. Even Saints like Saint John Maximovitch have served Divine Liturgy there. Every donation you make, no matter the size, is like an arrow that hits satan right where it counts. Let's get those arrows going! You can even make

CHAPTER SEVEN

a donation and ask for specific prayers on your or your family's behalf. I encourage everyone to do so.

After all, the monastics are praying for *all of us*. This ever-increasingly Godless world is against these spiritual warriors. These monks don't have an easy job. They are literally fighting the world for us. I remember hearing a spiritual nugget about monasticism when Serbian Hieromonk Father Serafim Baltic (who attended Holy Trinity Seminary, Jordanville) came to my home to do my Serbian Slava (my Slava is Saint Petka). One of my American friends who came to my Slava was asking him all sorts of questions. As I walked by, I overheard him tell her, we monks wear black, so you don't have to.

I will never forget the first time I traveled from my home in Nashville to the venerable Holy Trinity Monastery at Jordanville. When I heard the Monastery Bells ring, for a moment I forgot it was the twenty-first century. Time froze. It felt so ancient. I felt as if Saint Sava of Serbia or Saint Job of Pochaev could walk through the cathedral doors at any minute.

I am so grateful to Very Reverend Archimandrite Nektarios Serfes who advised me to make my first trip there. I explained my situation, and he knew I needed the ancient ethos of Orthodoxy found in this holy place! I believe there is no monastery quite like it in the United States. I needed the holy air there. Everything at Jordanville is completely immersed in the Kingdom of God. It's almost impossible not to feel this all-encompassing holiness!

Who would think visiting a monastery would bring me such happiness? You might think instead

CHAPTER SEVEN

The future of Orthodoxy: Holy Trinity Seminarians.
Please donate: https://hts.edu/support

that a tropical island trip would do the job. When the ten-year point of caring for Mama came, I simply could not get my cheerful self back. I felt like Eyore, woe is me. Where was my joy? I kept thinking about how Saint Seraphim of Sarov addressed everyone as "My Joy!" I wondered many a time how could he be so cheerful? Even after he was beaten up by robbers and his back remained hunched over for the rest of his life, the robbers could not take his joy and peace in Christ.

The vile spirit of the world had gotten to me. Hope, peace, and joy seemed far away. The sinful world had invariably confused me. It made me forget that God was *always* with me. I needed to

CHAPTER SEVEN

find the peace of God. I could not find it in my heart because of my worries. Even when I went to church and returned home, my despondency returned. My mother, on the other hand, seemed so serene and at one with God. She had regular monthly communion as she laid in bed day in and day out. I never saw a frown on her face. She had peace, but peace was far from me.

Thankfully, the good Lord found a way to get me to Jordanville. He met me right there inside my heart

Saint Seraphim always addressed everyone as "My Joy."
He knew God created us for the joy of the Heavenly Kingdom.

CHAPTER SEVEN

and instilled joy. I had an interaction with the living God through The Pochaev Icon and my anxiety and worries departed. Joy and beauty entered in. I met our Lord and Savior Jesus Christ right there, by way of His mother, in front of The Pochaev Icon at Jordanville. My heart found this peace because God and His saints are invisibly present at Jordanville. I thank God and the Mother of God for arranging my trip to Jordanville.

When we are troubled, help awaits. Sometimes you need to go to the big guns, like Jordanville, to soak in the The Kingdom of God. Even outside the services, if you walk quietly around the monastery grounds, you can feel it. I pray that all of you burdened with your own crosses will make the very same trip to seek the Kingdom of God for your life. How can any of us believers forget these words?

But seek ye first the Kingdom of God and His righteousness; and all these things shall be added unto you.
Matthew 6:33, KJV

God sees when we visit and support a monastery and seminary like Jordanville. Our souls benefit and reap eternal rewards by doing this. These are His chosen places. I sincerely hope that sometime, in the near future, each of you will make it your spiritual goal to visit Jordanville and experience its holiness first hand. You can start by ordering a blessed reproduction of The Pochaev Icon. Hang it in your prayer corner. Light your lampada before it. Ask the Mother of God to pray and help you make

CHAPTER SEVEN

*Above photo and following pages:
Processions with the Pochaev Icon of the Mother God, with
Monastics and Clergy at Jordanville.*

CHAPTER SEVEN

THE POCHAEV ICON • 225

CHAPTER SEVEN

226 • THE POCHAEV ICON

CHAPTER SEVEN

this trip possible! She will hear your holy petition. Keep praying. Be persistent like the widow we discussed earlier.

Before your visit, be sure to check out their website, **https://Jordanville.org**, for visitor information such as: guesthouses and monastery etiquette. You can also stay in nearby Herkimer or the lovely lakefront village of Cooperstown.

I recently asked His Grace Bishop Luke to write a few words for each of you to learn a little more about Jordanville's spiritual beauty. Please turn to the following pages to read His Grace, Bishop Luke's statement and reflection.

CHAPTER SEVEN

*His Grace, Bishop Luke of Syracuse,
Rector of Holy Trinity Seminary and Abbot of
Holy Trinity Monastery, Jordanville, New York*

STATEMENT FOR THE READERS OF THIS BOOK FROM HIS GRACE, BISHOP LUKE

As one drives through the rolling hills of the southern part of rural Herkimer County, one might be astonished to come upon buildings with golden cupolas and Russian Orthodox crosses. It is as if one had traveled to Russia. Indeed, one has arrived at a piece of holy Russia in the midst of rural upstate New York.

The Holy Trinity Monastery was founded in 1930 by Fr. Panteleimon Niznik, a monk who had immigrated from pre-revolutionary Russia to work in the factories, save money, and return home. However, he was overtaken by the upheaval of the Communist revolution and remained in the United States, becoming a monk and dedicating his life to his salvation.

It worked out that the Lord chose this humble monastery to become the spiritual center of the Russian diaspora and one of the most important centers of Eastern Orthodoxy in the New World. Contained within its confines are many precious relics and icons of the Church as well as a man's monastery and the only seminary of the Russian Orthodox Church Outside of Russia, as well as a very important museum of Russian history and culture.

In the main chapel of the monastery is contained the precious and very much venerated copy of The

STATEMENT

Pochaev Icon of the Most Holy Mother of God, a gift to the monastery from the very Pochaev Monastery in Ukraine, once one of the most important monastic houses of the former Russian Empire. It is regarded by the faithful as a miraculous icon in that many have been healed, both spiritually and physically, as witnessed by many gifts of gratitude which hang upon the icon.

Besides being a precious spiritual home to countless Orthodox Christians who travel to the monastery from all corners of the globe, the monastery, continuing in the tradition of Saint Job of Pochaev, the first abbot of the Pochaev Monastery, continues to work for the enlightenment of people, both Orthodox and non-Orthodox, who are seeking to find genuine Christianity in a world full of corruption and spiritual emptiness. In the monastery's baptistry, many are those who receive holy illumination in baptism. In our evil times, many young men choose to enter the monastic life and find their home in the monastery.

Monasteries in Russia have always been centers of pilgrimage, and so the Holy Trinity Monastery with its many holy objects and beautiful services, and most importantly with its publication of edifying books, strives to continue the legacy of Pochaev, under the protection of the Most Holy Virgin Mary, Whose holy icon guides and protects all those who come to Her.

His Grace Luke, Bishop of Syracuse,
Vicar of the Eastern America Diocese of the
Russian Orthodox Church Outside of Russia

STATEMENT

The original Pochaev Icon of the Mother of God is pictured here at the Monastery church at Ladomirova (now Svidnik District, Slovakia). This monastery was severely damaged in 1944 by Red Army air raids. Its monastic community ceased to exist in 1946. **Thankfully, the legacy of Pochaev, under the protection of the Most Holy Virgin Mary, continues on at Jordanville.**

STATEMENT

As I arrive at Pascha and the end of this book, I cross myself and say: Christ is Risen! Indeed, He is Risen! I joyfully reflect upon the words of the **Paschal Canon (Ode 9, Refrain 4):**

"The angel cried to Her who is full of grace: Rejoice, pure Virgin! And again I say, Rejoice! Thy Son has risen on the third day from the grave, and has raised the dead. Rejoice, you people!"

Little wonder Saint Seraphim of Sarov greeted every person he met by saying, "My Joy!" He absolutely knew the source of true joy! No matter what tribulation he endured, one thing is clear, true joy never left him! From generation to generation, our grace-filled Heavenly Mother continues to direct us all to Christ — our eternal joy!

By the grace of God, we have come together through this book to contemplate and once again be reminded of the spiritual greatness of the Theotokos. We have seen this greatness manifested through Her miracle-working Pochaev Icon. May we never forget to call upon our Ardent Intercessor for help in any life situation. I will continue to pray before this icon throughout my life and specifically ask that the Theotokos intercede on behalf of each reader.

STATEMENT

I conclude with my personal prayer to the Mother of God:

> Most wondrous Virgin and Mother of our Lord on High, You are the greatest of all the Saints and a miracle for us in our times of suffering. I thank you Most Holy Theotokos for helping me through difficult times and manifesting your love for all humanity through your miraculous Pochaev Icon. Please remember everyone who reads this book. Protect and save them Most Holy Mother of God. Forever guide them on the straight and narrow path to our Lord and Savior Jesus Christ. Enlighten our hearts, Theotokos, and please raise this prayer of mine to Your Son to save our souls. Amen.

Rejoice, O Praise of Pochaev, the Hope and Consolation of the world!

STATEMENT

The Jordanville Pochaev Icon of the Mother of God (without riza) The Pochaev Icon of the Mother of God is commemorated on the Friday of Bright Week, July 23/August 5, and September 8/21.

AKATHIST TO THE MOST-HOLY THEOTOKOS

*In honor of Her
Wonderworking Icon of Pochaev*

Kondak 1

O Chosen Leader of the Christian people

Their renowned Deliverance and Protection,

We the faithful bring our grateful songs of praise to thee, O Lady Theotokos:

And as thou doth possess imponderable depths of mercy,

Despise not the prayers that we offer before thy Wonderworking Image

For in the humility of our hearts we sing:

Rejoice, O praise of Pochaev, the Hope and Consolation of the world.

Ikos 1

Gabriel the Archangel was the first to proclaim, "Rejoice!" O Lady, when he announced to thee thy conception of the Son of God. Then at thy Most-glorious Dormition, all the Powers of Heaven raised their voice in ceaseless praise, "Rejoice!" How then, can we sinners dare to join our feeble voices to those of the bodiless hosts? But since thou art merciful and tenderhearted towards all that repent, we open our mouths with fear and with love as we dare to sing:

Rejoice, Unfathomable well of mercy.

Rejoice, O boundless sea of love.

Rejoice, O blessed refuge of the Christian people.

Rejoice, Invincible protectress of Pochaev.

Rejoice, For the Orthodox people are drawn to thee through thy love.

Rejoice, For thou doth dispel their every grief and sorrow.

Rejoice, For thine image, shining like a star, guides us along the way of life.

Rejoice, For the prayers fervently offered before her are speedily answered.

Rejoice, For thine appearance on the Mount of Pochaev has brought great comfort to thy people.

Rejoice, For the trace of thy footstep is upon that Hill.

Rejoice, For thou art the firm courage of the faithful.

Rejoice, For thou art the loving consolation of the weak.

Rejoice, O Praise of Pochaev, the Hope and Consolation of the world.

Kondak 2

Seeing thine appearance on the face of the hill in the wilderness of Pochaev as in a pillar of fire, the blessed fool Saint John the Barefoot tenderly kissed the trace of thy footprint upon the rock, and sprinkling himself with the water flowing from it, he sang to God: Alleluia!

Ikos 2

Pondering the imponderable mercy of thine appearance, O Lady, we affirm through our fervent supplications, that thou didst deign to establish a stronghold for Orthodoxy on the Mount of Pochaev as a defense against the Hagarites and then, against the onslaughts of the heretics. Therefore, our hearts overflow with the warm fervor of faith as we come before thee and we sing:

Rejoice, O confirmation of the True Faith.

Rejoice, Exposer of evil heresies.

AKATHIST

Rejoice, Fulfillment of the ancient prophecy of the Burning Bush;

Rejoice, Appearance to Christians in a pillar of fire.

Rejoice, For the Holy Youths foresaw thee as the dew in the fiery furnace.

Rejoice, For the water that flows from the trace of thy footprint proclaims thy healing grace.

Rejoice, For thine appearance brought great comfort to the land defiled by the Hagarites.

Rejoice, For the strength that we gain through thy many signs and miracles.

Rejoice, O help and refuge of monastics.

Rejoice, O bestower of wisdom upon the uninstructed.

Rejoice, O strength and courage of the weak.

Rejoice, O Quick-to-Hear the supplications of our repentance.

Rejoice, O Praise of Pochaev, the Hope and Consolation of the world.

Kondak 3

Thou didst reveal to us the power of thy grace, O

Lady, by choosing the place of thy blessed appearance to be the abode of this, thy Wonderworking Icon. Since her arrival over four hundred years ago, her presence has enriched the Mount of Pochaev. She was first brought there by Bishop Neophytus the Hellene, who while returning to Greece from Moscow, presented this image to the noble woman Anna as a blessing for her kindness towards him. She in turn, bequeathed her to the Monastery of Pochaev to the joy of all the people who sing to God: Alleluia!

Ikos 3

When this icon was in her house, the noble Anna witnessed the miraculous healing of her brother Phillip who had been blind from birth. She was then filled with a burning desire to proclaim thy glory and she built a stone Church at Pochaev dedicated in honor of thy Most-holy Dormition for the pious brotherhood where this, thy Wonderworking Icon is venerated to this day.

Rejoice, For bestowing upon us the rich treasure of thine Icon.

Rejoice, For blessing the land of Volyn' through the blessing of the Hierarch.

Rejoice, For turning away our souls from material riches.

Rejoice, For teaching us to sing the glory of God.

AKATHIST

Rejoice, For beholding thy wonders, our hearts rejoice to the heavens.

Rejoice, For standing in thy presence we stand before the gates of paradise.

Rejoice, For the Orthodox faithful are comforted while beholding thine image.

Rejoice, For the faithful are drawn to thee from all the ends of the earth.

Rejoice, For our faith is increased through thee.

Rejoice, For all our sorrows are erased through thee.

Rejoice, For thou art the earnest joy of monastics.

Rejoice, O profound comfort of all the faithful.

Rejoice, O Praise of Pochaev, the Hope and Consolation of the World.

Kondak 4

A furious storm was released by the heretics in their attack upon thy habitation, O Lady, and in their blasphemy, the Iconoclasts stole this, thy holy Icon away into captivity. But their sacrilege was finally put to an end by the wrath of God, for while the captors feasted in their depraved impiety like did Herod or Artaxerxes of old, and sought to defile thine image, they were struck down with a palsy for they knew not how to sing: Alleluia!

Ikos 4

When thy seventeen-year captivity in the hands of the heretics was finally brought to an end, and thy return to thy habitation from the prison of the blasphemers was finally at hand, the monks of Pochaev and all the faithful came out to greet thee in their gladness, they raised high their voices, and with joy they sang:

Rejoice, O refuge and haven of Christians.

Rejoice, Exposer of evil heresies.

Rejoice, For thou didst put the blasphemers to shame.

Rejoice, For thou didst not forsake the true abode of thy miraculous Icon.

Rejoice, For teaching us not to despair in sorrow.

Rejoice, For teaching us rather, to trust in the righteous Judgment of God.

Rejoice, For thou art the confirmation of the Orthodox Faith.

Rejoice, For through thee has the entire universe come to know Wisdom made flesh.

Rejoice, For emulating the longsuffering forbearance of God.

Rejoice, For teaching thy people to learn patience in affliction.

Rejoice, For the proud are taught humility through thee.

Rejoice, O Praise of Pochaev, the Hope and Consolation of the world.

Kondak 5

To those seeking salvation thou dost appear as a shining star overflowing with the Mercy of God leading them forward to the Sun of Righteousness. For in thy earthly life, O Lady, thou didst show thyself to be the Intercessor for thy people before thy Son in Cana of Galilee. And now, after thy glorious Dormition and Assumption into Heaven, thou dost ever pray before thy Son for all the faithful who come to thee from the ends of the earth, bringing their prayers to Him that they might receive from Him His healing bounty and sing to God: Alleluia!

Ikos 5

When the people behold the river of miraculous healings pouring forth from the Mountain of Pochaev from the days of old even unto this day, they are filled with the ardent desire to repent of their past sins and thus attain salvation, and they sing this song to thee:

Rejoice, O giver of sight to the blind and the healer of the sick.

Rejoice, Remover of demonic possessions.

Rejoice, For wondrously freeing the captive monk from his prison.

Rejoice, For raising the infant Symeon from his deathbed at the Elder's prayer.

Rejoice, for these signs and miracles are shown us even to this day.

Rejoice, For thou dost grant healing through thine holy Image in these latter days.

Rejoice, For thy healing Icons are found throughout the world.

Rejoice, For through them the faithful are filled with spiritual treasures.

Rejoice, For thou art the boast of the Orthodox people.

Rejoice, For unbelievers are also drawn to thee.

Rejoice, O hope of us mortals.

Rejoice, O joy of the bodiless hosts.

Rejoice, O Praise of Pochaev, the Hope and Consolation of the world.

Kondak 6

The Hagarites themselves became proclaimers of thy glory. O Most-pure Virgin, when they beheld thee together with the Venerable Igumen Job defending the Monastery of Pochaev from their savage attack. Not realizing their folly, they fired their arrows upon thee and were themselves smitten dead by their return flight. Seeing this power displayed by thee. O Lady, the infidels forsook their folly and with faith they cried: Alleluia!

Ikos 6

Beholding thine appearance, O Lady, above the Mountain of Pochaev in answer to the prayers of the brotherhood before this, thine holy Image and before the relics of the venerable Job, and witnessing thy power in the destruction of their comrades, the army of the Hagarites took to flight in panic. Seeing this, the faithful cried aloud to thee with joy:

Rejoice, Ever-vigilant guardian of the Christian people.

Rejoice, O our champion and defender.

AKATHIST

Rejoice, O protectress that defeats our impious enemies.

Rejoice, For bringing them to repentance.

Rejoice, For through thee our enemies are amazed by our salvation.

Rejoice, For the holy Angels and the righteous departed fall down before thee in reverence.

Rejoice, For revealing the Venerable Job as an intercessor for our prayers.

Rejoice, For through thee the faithful no longer fear the hour of death.

Rejoice, For the former Hagarites who returned as monks to Pochaev.

Rejoice O pure and constant exposition of the Truth.

Rejoice, O good instructor of those that were lost.

Rejoice, O Praise of Pochaev, the Hope and Consolation of the world.

Kondak 7

Wishing to enflame the hearts of Christian believers with the zeal for Life Everlasting, the Most-holy Theotokos, through Her miracles, heals the sick, chases away demons, frees those held captive, and raises the dead so that we might come to know the Power of God. Let us therefore, lay aside all earthly cares and let us stir our souls to earnestly and ceaselessly sing to God: Alleluia!

Ikos 7

New and terrible travails aggrieved thy holy habitation at Pochaev when it and the entire land of Volyn' were deviously torn away from Orthodoxy and thrust into the clutches of heretics. Finally after one hundred and ten years the Orthodox Christians prevailed, and when the Orthodox monks returned to thy monastery and revealed the relics of Saint Job for veneration, they fell before this, thy holy Image, and they sang:

Rejoice, O defender of Orthodoxy.

Rejoice, Exposer of evil heresies.

Rejoice, For thou didst not forsake thy habitation.

Rejoice, For teaching us the fear of God.

Rejoice, For through thine intercessions, the land of Volyn' was returned to the Orthodox faith.

Rejoice, For throughout the ages heretics were enlightened by thee.

AKATHIST

Rejoice, For even the faithless are taught to pray before this, thy holy image.

Rejoice, For the Orthodox faithful are called to pray at thy Monastery to this day.

Rejoice, For she is forever the praise of the faithful.

Rejoice, For she calls to herself those who have forsaken repentance.

Rejoice, For she returns to the Church those who had lost their faith.

Rejoice, For she beckons those in darkness into the Light of Truth.

Rejoice, O Praise of Pochaev, the Hope and Consolation of the world.

Kondak 8

We behold thy marvelous wonders, O Theotokos, for we see the physically infirm receive healing as they venerate this, thy holy image; we see those torn by spiritual passions washed clean by this, thy sacred icon. We see renewal, and True faith in God restored, as our hearts overflow with love we cry out to Him: Alleluia!

Ikos 8

I am totally unworthy and my entire being is fraught

AKATHIST

with sin! I am so immersed in the secular cares of this world, that I ignore my soul completely! But beholding thy holy image before me and seeing with my very own eyes the illumination being bestowed upon the countless number of people standing here with me, each one being guided upon the path of salvation, in the gladness of my heart I sing:

Rejoice, Endless source of mercies,

Rejoice, O treasury of purity.

Rejoice, O intercessor, bringing our prayers before thy Son.

Rejoice, For not despising the prayers of us sinners.

Rejoice, For through thee many escape the sin of despair.

Rejoice, For after falling into sin we are able to get up again by calling on thy name.

Rejoice, For the heresy of iconoclasm has been thoroughly put to shame by thee.

Rejoice, For the true faith of Orthodoxy has been restored to the land of Volyn' through thee.

Rejoice, For teaching us to forgive our enemies.

Rejoice, For leading our souls to embrace chastity.

AKATHIST

Rejoice, For pouring thy love into our hearts.

Rejoice, For thou art the hope and longing of our souls.

Rejoice, O Praise of Pochaev, the Hope and Consolation of the world.

Kondak 9

Thou didst quickly forgive the repentant people of the land of Volyn' for any offense they had made while struggling under the yoke of heresy, O Lady, and thou didst immediately restore to them the streams of miraculous healings flowing from thy Wonderworking Icon and the trace of thy footprint. These gifts are now given freely to all, who come before God with repentance in their hearts and with unshakeable faith in thine intercession cry to Him: Alleluia!

Ikos 9

Once again, O Lady, thou didst show us the bounties of thy mercy when thy people were restored to the Orthodox Faith: the blind received their sight and the lame received their strength when they called upon thee in prayer. Likewise, the Lutheran woman was immediately healed when she cried out to thee for help; and having received healing she venerated thee with kisses and accepted the True Faith. Like her then, let us sing:

AKATHIST

Rejoice, O constant advocate for us mortals.

Rejoice, For thine entreaties before the King of Heaven.

Rejoice, For converting the Protestant woman through thy healing.

Rejoice, O confirmation of Orthodoxy for all the people.

Rejoice, For the many victories of the Orthodox over their enemies.

Rejoice, For the numerous people who converted to Orthodoxy for thy sake.

Rejoice, For all the people lift their eyes to thee in prayer.

Rejoice, For they beg thee to pray for the repose of the departed.

Rejoice, For delivering us from all the cares of this world.

Rejoice, For granting us the strength to endure the travails of this life.

Rejoice, Firm defender of Christian soldiers.

Rejoice, For teaching us to withstand the attacks of the demons.

Rejoice, O Praise of Pochaev, the Hope and Consolation of the world.

Kondak 10

Seeking the salvation of a simple woman blinded by false teachings, O Most-pure Theotokos, thou didst move her young granddaughter, blind in her eyes from birth but illumined with the light of Orthodoxy, to implore her to bring her to venerate this, thy holy Image on the Mountain of Pochaev. And when they came before thee, O Lady, the blind girl was healed and her grandmother was taught to proclaim the Orthodox Faith and she sang to God: Alleuia!

Ikos 10

Thou art the invincible fortress of the True Faith, O Lady, for all the attacks of the deceitful heretics are repulsed by thy strong and mighty bastions. Likewise, O true Theotokos, thou art the safe haven of all the Orthodox who call upon thee in faith, for the words of heresy fall silent in our ears and with grateful thanks in our hearts we ceaselessly sing:

Rejoice, O joy and consolation of Christians.

Rejoice, Glory and honor of Angels.

Rejoice, Protection against the evils of heresy.

AKATHIST

Rejoice, For in remembering thy mercies we turn our minds to God.

Rejoice, For calling the Apostles to be with thee at thy Dormition.

Rejoice, For calling countless multitudes of the faithful to be with thee on the day of thy Feast.

Rejoice, For after enduring hardships, the faithful find a sweet repose through thee.

Rejoice, For the weak in spirit are inspired to seek the same reward through thee.

Rejoice, For in thy mercy, the monastics find a haven from all earthly temptations.

Rejoice, For they are frightened awake from the horror of sin.

Rejoice, O precious diadem of the Church of Christ.

Rejoice, O stalwart defender of the land of Volyn.

Rejoice, O Praise of Pochaev, the Hope and Consolation of the world.

Kondak 11

Songs of praise glorifying thy miracles have encircled the globe, O Lady, ceaselessly rising, as sweet incense, unto the heavens from the unworthy lips of faithful Christians. Turn not away from us, we pray thee, and grant unto us the bounties of repentance as we sing to God: Alleluia!

Ikos 11

To the dying man of Bessarabia thou didst appear both as a lamp shining upon his earthly life and as a beacon guiding him safely home unto life everlasting, O Lady; for as he was breathing his last breath, his lips tasted the waters of thy healing Pochaev spring, and straightway, he arose. Beholding this, his family with fear and love cried to thee:

Rejoice, O restoration of the sick.

Rejoice, For hearing the prayers of those in sorrows.

Rejoice, For death approaching is vanquished.

Rejoice, For we have been granted a firm and unshakable faith.

Rejoice, For we see with our own eyes the Announcement of Gabriel.

Rejoice, For indeed, all generations do call thee blessed.

Rejoice, For thou has sanctified Pochaev as thy divine abode.

Rejoice, For Pochaev has become a second Nazareth.

Rejoice, For not despising any prayer of supplication.

Rejoice, For graciously accepting the prayers of all.

Rejoice, For granting us streams of healing grace.

Rejoice, For turning us onto the path of salvation.

Rejoice O Praise of Pochaev, the Hope and Consolation of the world.

Kondak 12

May the grace of thy mercies and the bountiful healings which stream from thy holy Icon, O Lady, not flow uselessly into our souls hardened by the arrogance of our sins; but as thou doth possess the power to raise even the dead, awaken then the deadened condition of our souls, and fill our hearts with good things, that we may learn to despise the sweet allure of sin and cry to God: Alleluia!

Ikos 12

Standing before thee and praising the miracles and wonders that thou hast shown to us on the Mountain of Pochaev, we beseech thee, O Lady: Turn not thy face away from us, but in thy mercy grant unto us, and to all that come before thee, the fulfillment of every good desire so that the entire world may sing:

AKATHIST

Rejoice, Steadfast advocate for us before thy Son.

Rejoice, Who softens the heart of the Righteous God.

Rejoice, For giving us the glorious victory of faith.

Rejoice, For filling our hearts with thy love.

Rejoice, For showing to us thy miracles of old.

Rejoice, For revealing the Mountain of Pochaev as a new Mount Sinai.

Rejoice, For bringing forth God Incarnate from thy womb.

Rejoice, For bringing mankind closer to God through thy holy intercessions.

Rejoice, For granting us thine Icon as a herald of Salvation.

Rejoice, For leaving us the trace of thy footprint as a source of healing waters.

Rejoice, For watching over us, thy servants, from the heights of heaven.

Rejoice, For guiding us onto the path of righteousness.

Rejoice, O Praise of Pochaev, the Hope and Consolation of the world.

Kondak 13

O All-praised Mother of Christ our God, who hath lovingly adopted as thine own all the generations of Christian people! Though we sinners know we are unable to praise thee worthily, but being wounded by thy love, we lift up our eyes to behold this, thy holy and Wonderworking Image, and we beseech thee: Do not abandon us thy children to the storms and passions of our desires, for we firmly believe in thine intercession, and with faith we sing to Christ, thy son: Alleluia!

(This Kondak is sung three times, then Ikos 1, and Kondak 1 are repeated in order)

Ikos 1

Gabriel the Archangel was the first to proclaim, "Rejoice!" O Lady, when he announced to thee thy conception of the Son of God. Then at thy Most-glorious Dormition, all the Powers of Heaven raised their voice in ceaseless praise, "Rejoice!" How then, can we sinners dare to join our feeble voices to those of the bodiless hosts? But since thou art merciful and tenderhearted towards all that repent, we open our mouths with fear and with love as we dare to sing:

Rejoice, Unfathomable well of mercy.

Rejoice, O boundless sea of love.

Rejoice, O blessed refuge of the Christian people.

AKATHIST

Rejoice, Invincable protectress of Pochaev.

Rejoice, For the Orthodox people are drawn to thee through thy love.

Rejoice, For thou doth dispel their every grief and sorrow.

Rejoice, For thine Image, shining like a star, guides us along the way of life.

Rejoice, For the prayers fervently offered before her are speedily answered.

Rejoice, For thine appearance on the Mount of Pochaev has brought great comfort to thy people.

Rejoice, For the trace of thy footstep is upon that Hill.

Rejoice, For thou art the firm courage of the faithful.

Rejoice, For thou art the loving consolation of the weak.

Rejoice, O Praise of Pochaev, the Hope and Consolation of the world.

Kondak 1 (Tone 8)

O Chosen Leader of the Christian people.

AKATHIST

Their renowned Deliverance and Protection,

We the faithful bring our grateful songs of praise to thee, O Lady Theotokos:

And as thou doth possess imponderable depths of mercy,

Despise not the prayers that we offer before thy Wonderworking Image.

For in the humility of our hearts we sing:

Rejoice, O Praise of Pochaev, the Hope and Consolation of the world.

Prayer to the Most-Holy Theotokos

We sinners stand before thee in prayer, O Mother of God, fully understanding the wonder of thy miracles shown at thy holy Monastery of Pochaev, and fully realizing the oppressive depths of our transgressions. And we know, O Lady, we know it is not right for us sinners to ask for anything except that the Righteous Judge would remit our lawless sins. Everything that we have suffered in this life; all the tribulations, sickness and distress, are the fruits of the downfall into sin, and are permitted to transpire by God so that we may correct our sinful ways. These are all brought down upon us, His servants, by His True and Righteous Judgement. Therefore, in our sorrow, we come and stand before thee begging thine intercessions, O most-holy Lady; we come in the profound humility of our heart, and we call upon thee: Remember not all our sins and transgression, O Good one. But rather, stand before thy Son and God and stretch out thy Most-pure hands before Him and plead on our behalf, that all the sins we have committed be forgiven; that He not turn His Face away from us, His servants, for all the failed promises that we have given; that He not take away from us His Grace, that leadeth all souls to salvation. Yea, O Lady, supplicate for us unto our salvation, and do not be dismayed by our lack of strength; but rather look down and behold our groanings as we stand in prayer before thy Wonderworking Icon in our sorrow and our pain. Enlighten our minds with tender thoughts; strengthen thou our faith; and allow us to taste the sweetest gifts of Love! For with these gifts, O Pure one, will our souls be brought unto salvation; and by protecting our souls from slothfulness and despair, we may be delivered from all our petty and foolish sins, the conceit and arrogance of pride, the scornings of our fellow man and from all infirmities. Grant peace and tranquility to this Christian Habitation, O Lady, through the power of thy prayer; Confirm and strengthen the Orthodox Faith in this our land and throughout the world. Let not the holy Catholic and apostolic Church diminish; preserve unchanged unto all ages the rules established by the holy Fathers; and save all those who come before thee from the ravenous jaws of hell. Likewise, bring back our brethren who have fallen into heresy or have forsaken the grace of salvation

AKATHIST

through their folly and their sin. Bring them back into repentance and back into the True Faith, so that together with us, they might venerate this, thy holy Wonderworking Icon and confess thine intercession and thy might. And make us worthy O Most-pure Lady Theotokos to behold the victory of Truth in this, our lifetime on the earth; make us worthy to be partakers of the Blessed Joy before the hour of our death; that we may together with the Angels and the Prophets, the Apostles, and all the Saints praise thy marvelous mercy and ascribe glory, honor and worship to the Holy Trinity, Father, Son, and Holy Spirit, now and ever, and unto the ages of ages. Amen.

(Now, the Troparon, Kontakion and Magnification, in order)

*Troparion to the
Pochaev Icon of the Mother of God*

(Tone 4)

We come as humble and sinful before the Theotokos

Falling down before Her Wondrous Image from the mount of Pochaev

With humility we gaze upon her and we fervently pray,

From the depths of our soul, we cry to our Lady and Queen:

AKATHIST

O Most Wondrous Virgin, Mother of our Lord on High,

Who from ancient times hast taken the Monastery of Pochaev as Her habitation

Confirm this land in Orthodoxy and keep her in peace

And save us all who tearfully pray before this, thy Most-Pure Image,

Turn not away from us, thy servants, whose only hope is in thee. Glory…, now and ever…Amen.

*Kontakion to the
Pochaev Icon of the Mother of God*

O Chosen Leader, who hath chosen for Herself the mount of Pochaev as Her dwelling place,

We thy servants sing these hymns of praise to thee, O Theotokos:

Since from ancient times thou hast glorified this God-bearing habitation

Through the dispensation of thy healing footprint and the presence of thy Holy and Wonderworking Image

Therefore, as once thou didst save thy habitation from the invasion of the Hagarites,

Deliver us from every sorrow and affliction through thine intercessions, who cry aloud to thee:

Rejoice, O Praise of Pochaev, our Hope and Consolation!

Magnification

We magnify thee, O Most-holy Virgin, and we honor thy precious Image, which of old thou didst glorify at Pochaev.

This Akathist is a translation based on the original Church Slavonic from Saint Tikhon's Seminary Press, ©2002. Commemorating the occasion of Her historic visit to the Monastery of Saint Tikhon of Zadonsk, South Canaan, Pennsylvania, USA (May 24-27, 2002).

FROM THE AUTHOR

AUTHOR

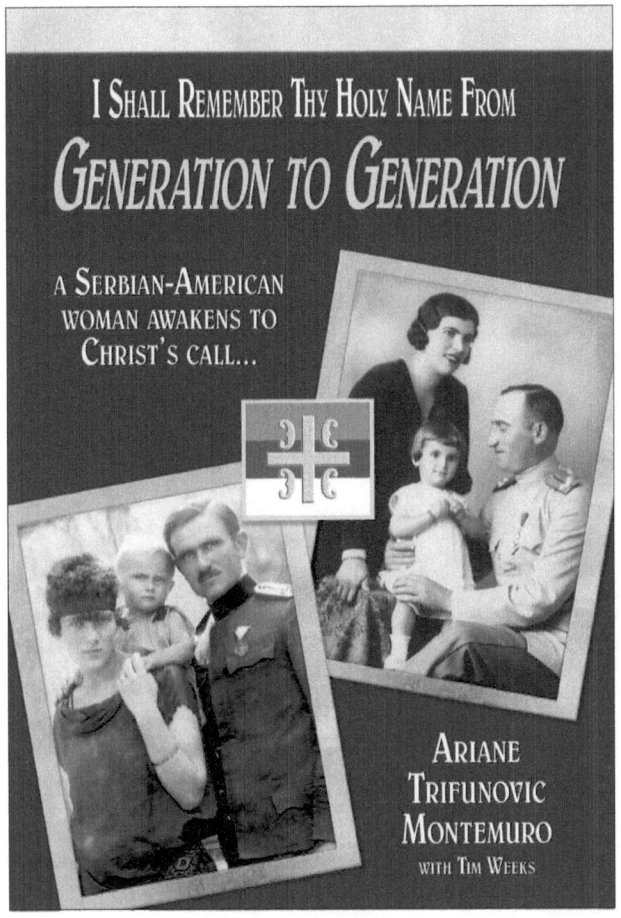

Ariane's books are available through all major online booksellers including Amazon at https://www.amazon.com/.

AUTHOR

Ariane's books are available through all major online booksellers including Amazon at https://www.amazon.com/.

AUTHOR

Ariane's books are available through all major online booksellers including Amazon at https://www.amazon.com/.

AUTHOR

Ariane's books are available through all major online booksellers including Amazon at https://www.amazon.com/.

AUTHOR

*The author in her art studio pictured with some of her
Orthodox Christian original oil paintings.
She is holding an oil painting she recently completed of the
Russian Orthodox Church of the Nativity of Christ and Saint
Nicholas the Wonderworker, in Florence, Italy.
Ariane's dream is to one day translate her books into different
languages to inspire everyone, everywhere, to strive to love and
live in communion with God.
Framed reproductions of some of her art can be found
on Ebay at: https://ebay.to/3EA2VYT.*

AUTHOR

*The author and her beloved husband Tony,
who helped make this book possible.*

*Most Holy Theotokos of Pochaev, remember my husband Tony in
your intercessory prayers! May God grant him many years!*

www.ingramcontent.com/pod-product-compliance
Lightning Source LLC
Chambersburg PA
CBHW060516080526
44586CB00012B/505